THE CAMPAIGN OF
The Spanish Armada

THE CAMPAIGN OF

The Spanish Armada

PETER KEMP

Facts On File Publications
New York, New York ● Oxford, England

Published in North America in 1988
by Facts On File, Inc., 460 Park Avenue South,
New York, N.Y. 10016

Library of Congress Cataloging-in-Publication Data

Kemp, Peter
 The campaign of the Spanish Armada.

 Includes index.
 1. Armada, 1588. 2. Great Britain—History, Naval—
Tudors, 1485–1603. 3. Spain—History—Philip II, 1556–
1598. I. Title.
DA360.K46   988   942.05′5   87-19637

ISBN 0-8160-1828-6

Filmset in Great Britain by BAS Printers Limited, Over Wallop, Hampshire
Printed and bound in Spain by Heraclio Fournier SA, Vitoria

10 9 8 7 6 5 4 3 2 1

Title page: *Ships of the Spanish Armada lying in the River Tagus off
Lisbon. The galleon on the right shows the typical high aftercastle of
Spanish warship design of the period.*

Page 6: *Spanish galleons assembling for the expedition to the Azores in
1582 where Don Antonio, pretender to the throne of Portugal, had set
himself up as king with French support.*

Contents

For Peggy. Dear comrade and wife. In love and remembrance.

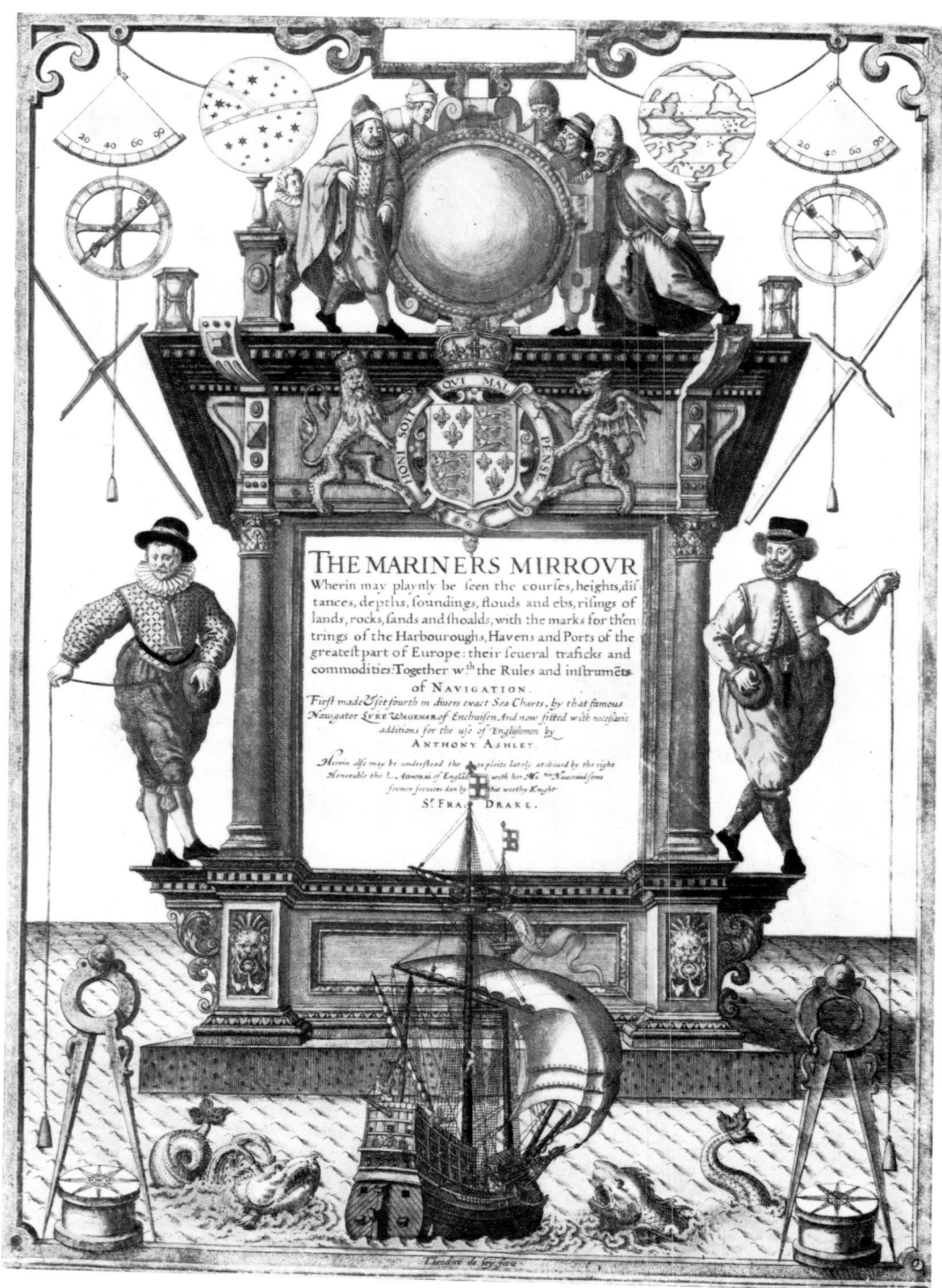

THE MARINERS MIRROVR

Wherin may playnly be seen the courses, heights, distances, depths, soundings, flouds and ebs, risings of lands, rocks, sands and shoalds, with the marks for thentrings of the Harbouroughs, Havens and Ports of the greatest part of Europe: their seueral traficks and commodities: Together wᵗʰ the Rules and instrumēts of NAVIGATION.

First made & set foorth in diuers exact Sea Charts, by that famous Nauigator LVKE WAGENAR of Enchuisen. And now fitted with necessarie additions for the use of Englishmen by ANTHONY ASHLEY.

Herein also may be understood the exploits lately atchiued by the right Honorable the L. Admiral of England, with her Mᵗⁱᵉ Nauie and some former seruices don by that worthy Knight Sʳ FRA. DRAKE.

Ilenderic de soy fora

Foreword

The campaign of the Spanish Armada in 1588 was one of the great climacterics of European history. Its influence reached far beyond the boundaries of Europe itself, stretching across the Atlantic Ocean to the Spanish colonial territories in the Americas and across the Indian Ocean to the Portuguese domination of India and the Far East. It took many years to reach its full zenith, both in Europe and across the oceans. There can be no serious question, however, that the defeat of the Armada in July/August 1588 destroyed thereafter the *status quo* in Europe and the rest of the world.

It would be a misreading of history to look upon this campaign solely in the light of a struggle between the forces of Reformation and Counter-Reformation. Certainly the Pope did, and certainly Philip of Spain gloried in his reputation as the champion of Roman Catholicism, but more lay behind Philip's 'Enterprise of England' than the defeat of Protestantism in England. Philip's eyes had long been on his American possessions as the main and inexhaustible source of Spanish wealth; after his accession to the throne of Portugal in 1581 he could also turn his eyes to the East as yet another source of prodigious wealth. The threat to a peaceful exploitation by Spain of both East and West lay primarily in English hands with the growing ferocity of their raids, or 'reprisals', into waters which Philip considered his exclusive property, and moreover raids to which Elizabeth invariably contributed one or more of her own warships.

It would be an equal misreading of history to suggest that the result of the Armada defeat was suddenly to transfer a dominance of European sea power from Spain to England. It is true that until 1588 Spain was recognized as the dominant naval power in Europe and that after 1588 a question mark hung over that assumption. In fact, even before the Armada sailed from Spain, Elizabethan England was already a considerable sea power; that she was not so recognized in Europe was because in recent history there had been little on which to judge her naval standing. The memory was still fresh of the Battle of Lepanto in 1571 in which the Spanish galleys had played a glorious part, and at Terçeira in 1582 a Spanish fleet had scattered a French attempt to establish the pretender Don Antonio in the Azores as a challenge to the disputed throne of Portugal. In both battles the Spanish admiral had been the Marquis of Santa Cruz, and he was still very much alive. His reputation as a fighting admiral shone as brightly as that of the Duke of Parma as Europe's most brilliant general. But about the only English naval name known in Europe was that of Francis Drake, widely regarded as a corsair and only very recently enlisted into the English navy.

Opposite: The title page of Anthony Ashley's The Mariners Mirrour, *depicting the contemporary dress of seamen and the navigational instruments of the day. The Mariners Mirrour was a translation of a Dutch sea atlas and was published in England in 1588.*

Below: The title page of Pedro de Medina's Regimiento de Navegacion, *one of the early Spanish manuals of navigation, published at Seville in 1552.*

Sea power is an elusive and largely indefinable will-o'-the-wisp. It takes years of endeavour and dedication to reach its full potential. So it was with England. Although her navy could take considerable pride in its achievement of 1588, England was to take another century of growth, of trial, of battle, before bringing home the full fruits of the defeat of the Spanish Armada. But the Armada campaign polarized the challenge to Spanish sea power and proved to Europe that the great trade routes across the oceans were open to those prepared to fight for them. Within a dozen or so years of the Armada battle not only England but five other European nations had formed their own East India companies to exploit the trade in the East.

Fleets of ships in those days were a mixture of 'royal' ships, those owned directly by the kings and queens of the various nations, and armed merchant ships, some taken up temporarily for a specific war purpose and paid for by their royal charterers, others offered by their merchant owners in a spirit of patriotism or in the hope of some reward in the shape of plunder of captured enemies. Inevitably such fleets included a large variety of ships with a wide list of type names which mean little to us today, such as carracks, galleons, galleasses, barges, hulks, urcas, hoys, balyngers, pinnaces, etc. I have tried to avoid as much as possible the use of such type names in order to simplify the text, preferring to describe the principal royal ships as galleons or galleasses as the case may be, and all the privately owned ships as merchant ships. It should be appreciated that several of the merchant ships were large, well-armed, frequently built on galleon lines, and not greatly short of the royal ships in their fighting capacity. It should also be appreciated that although the royal ships on both sides are called galleons or galleasses, a Spanish galleon was a very different ship from an English one. Spanish galleons were built with high sides and a welldeck amidships between towering castles forward and aft; the English galleon lay lower in the water with a flush deck, the forecastle much cut down in size and moved some distance aft behind a beakhead.

Any reading of the contemporary English and Spanish papers of the campaign reveals a ten day difference in dates, the difference between Old Style and New Style, or the Augustan and Gregorian calendars. Pope Gregory XIII had proclaimed his calendar in 1582 and almost the whole of western Europe had adopted it by 1587 with the exception of England. It would be possible, as an example, to write the date of the first meeting of the two fleets in the English Channel in 1588 as July $\frac{21}{31}$, the 21st being the Augustan and the 31st the Gregorian date. I have used the Gregorian date throughout both to simplify this account of the campaign and also to bring it into line with the calendar which we all use today, although in direct quotations from letters and despatches I have added the New Style date in square brackets to the original written date. Also in direct quotations I have occasionally inserted in square brackets a word or two to explain any possible ambiguities in the originals.

I am indebted to the Council of the Navy Records Society for permission to quote from its publications, a collection of volumes expertly edited and quite invaluable to the naval historian. Documents in Crown copyright appear by permission of the Controller of H.M.S.O. I am also deeply grateful to the many individuals who have assisted this project in one way or another, particularly to my old friends Richard Hough, John Bridges, and Dr John Peters, all of whom gave the manuscript a thorough and constructive reading much to its advantage. I also wish to thank Caroline Lucas for all the work she put into the picture research, with such happy results.

Morning prayer on board a Spanish caravel during the reign of Charles V. The coastal detail suggests that the ship is lying in the port of Corunna on the northern coast of Spain.

Omine maria tua mihi aperias. Et
nauis mea annunciabit laudem tuã.
Deus in nauigationem meam intende: Do
mine ad nauigandum me adiuta. Gloria pa
tri et filio et spiritu sancto. Sicut erat in prin
cipio et nunc et semper et in secula seculorum.
Amen. Alleluya. Inuitatorium Aue Maria
Lucida stella maris. Psalmus.

Shetland Is.

Fair Isle
Orkney Is.

SCOTLAND

Tobermory

Giant's Causeway
Inishowen Head
Glennagiveny Bay

Erris Head
Achill Head

Londonderry

Firth of Forth
Edinburgh

NORTH SEA

IRELAND
Dublin

IRISH SEA

The Blaskets

Cape Clear

ENGLAND
Great Yarmouth
Harwich
London
Chatham
Dover

HOLLAND

Flushing
Antwerp
Maastricht
Brussels

Plymouth

Scilly Is.

ENGLISH CHANNEL

Cherbourg

Calais

Le Havre
Paris

Ushant

Chartres

Blois

FRANCE

BAY OF BISCAY

La Rochelle

Coutras

Genoa

Cape Finisterre

Corunna
Santander
Bayonne

Vigo

ITALY
Rome

Naples

SPAIN

El Escurial
Madrid

PORTUGAL

Tagus

Peniche

Cascais
Cape Roca
Lisbon

Cape St. Vincent

Lagos
Sagres

Sanlúcar la Mayor
Seville

Cartagena

MEDITERRANEAN SEA

Cadiz

Chronology

1554	Philip, son and heir of Charles V, King of Spain and Holy Roman Emperor, marries Mary Tudor, Queen of England.
1555	Charles V resigns his sovereignty of the Netherlands in favour of his son Philip.
1556	Charles V abdicates. Philip succeeds to the throne of Spain and her European possessions of Naples and Sicily, the Duchy of Milan, and Burgundy, and also to her possessions in the West Indies and in North and South America.
1558	Death of Mary Tudor. Elizabeth succeeds to the throne of England.
1567	Philip sends an army into the Netherlands to enforce the Roman Catholic faith.
1568	Hawkins's third voyage to the West Indies ends in disaster at San Juan de Ulloa but provides the genesis of the new English design of the low-charged warship.
1577	William the Silent, Prince of Orange, acknowledged as leader of the whole of the Netherlands, pledges to expel the Spaniards. Elizabeth provides a financial subsidy to assist the Dutch.
1578	Philip appoints Alexander Farnese, Duke of Parma, as Governor-General of the Netherlands.
1580	Death of Henry, King of Portugal. Don Antonio occupies Lisbon and proclaims himself King.
1581	Don Antonio is defeated by a Spanish army and Philip of Spain is crowned as King of Portugal.
1584	William the Silent is assassinated at Ghent. Elizabeth sends an English army under the Earl of Leicester to assist the Dutch revolt.
1585	The Marquis of Santa Cruz is made Captain-General of the Ocean Sea and appointed to command the Spanish fleet for the invasion of England.
1585–6	The Indies Voyage. Drake leads an expedition, to which Elizabeth contributes two of her royal ships, against Spanish trade in the West Indies.

1587	Execution of Mary Stuart, Queen of Scotland and Elizabeth's heir to the throne of England.
1587	The raid on Cadiz. Drake leads an expedition of 23 ships, including four royal warships and two pinnaces, in a voyage of destruction on the coast of Spain. The *San Felipe*, a Portuguese carrack returning from the East Indies with an immensely rich cargo, is captured.
1588 January	Elizabeth mobilizes the English fleet.
9 February	Death of the Marquis of Santa Cruz. Philip appoints the Duke of Medina Sidonia to command the Armada.
28–30 May	The Armada sails from Lisbon bound for the English Channel but is scattered by gales and puts into Corunna to repair damage.
June	Howard is ordered to join Drake at Plymouth.
17 July	Howard and Drake sail with the English fleet to attack the Armada in Corunna but are forced to return by contrary winds.
21 July	The Armada sails from Corunna bound for the English Channel.
29 July	The Armada is sighted off the Devon coast.
30 July	The English fleet works its way out of Plymouth Sound against a head wind.
31 July	The battle off Plymouth.
2 August	The battle of Portland.
4 August	The battle off the Isle of Wight.
6 August	Both fleets anchor in Calais Roads. Seymour's squadron from the Downs joins the English fleet.
7 August	English fireships attack the Armada. The Spanish ships cut their cables and put to sea.
8 August	The battle of Gravelines.
9 August	The Armada, too demoralized to face another action against the English fleet, steers north to make its way home to Spain around Scotland and Ireland.
1589	Drake's expedition to Lisbon.

1 European Background

Perhaps the seeds of the defeat of the Spanish Armada were sown, quite unwittingly, by Charles V, the Holy Roman Emperor, on 25 October 1555, in the Hall of the Golden Fleece in Brussels, when he formally resigned his sovereignty of the Netherlands to his son Philip. Of all his great European empire, he had most loved the Netherlands. 'Gentlemen,' he said, addressing the representatives of the Estates, 'you must not be astonished if, old and feeble as I am in all my members, and also in the love I bear you, I shed some tears.' His love was reciprocated, and many of the thousand deputies who listened to their sovereign's speech also shed some tears.

Their love and respect for the father did not descend to the son. Charles had governed the separate provinces of the Netherlands with skill and tolerance, seldom trying to force his own Catholic religion on those dour Protestants in the most northerly of his kingdoms and encouraging a reasonable measure of self-government through provincial Diets. But whatever virtues his son Philip may have possessed, they did not include religious tolerance. Like much of the rest of his generation, Philip was convinced that unity of religion was indispensable to the maintenance of the authority of the State and it was that conviction which ultimately forced him to become a persecutor. The activities of the Inquisition in trying to enforce the universal embrace of Catholicism served only to harden the obstinacy of the Dutch and finally drive them into outright revolt. The Netherlands, which under wiser rule might have been a valuable bulwark in Philip's future war against England, became instead a running sore in the Spanish economy and a heavy millstone around Philip's own neck.

It was, perhaps, not all Philip's fault. His father had impressed on him a deep sense of the high destiny to which he had been born, and had opened up a great inheritance through a series of diplomatic marriages, using his relations to form useful alliances. One of these alliances, of which Charles had the greatest hope, was his arrangement of his son's marriage to Mary Tudor, Queen of England, in 1554. If Mary should produce an heir this might lead to a firm union between Spain and England.

England was the great prize. A Spanish presence there would surround France and force her into the Spanish orbit. Philip's first act following their marriage was to persuade Mary to join Spain in a war against France, a disastrous adventure that ended in England's loss of Calais, her toehold in northern France. It led, too, to a wide disenchantment in England with Mary's Spanish marriage and its implications, and the bad blood created resulted in the widespread burnings of Protestants and the Queen's sobriquet of Bloody Mary.

Charles, old and tired, abdicated in 1556 and Philip came into his full inheritance.

Charles V, King of Spain and Holy Roman Emperor, resigning the sovereignty of the Netherlands in favour of his son Philip. The ceremony was held in the Hall of the Golden Fleece in Brussels in 1555.

William, Prince of Orange, known as William the Silent. He was elected by the states of the Netherlands to lead the Dutch rebellion against Spanish occupation. In 1584 he was assassinated on the staircase of his house at Delft.

He found himself not only King of Spain and her American possessions but also of Naples and Sicily, of Burgundy, and of the Duchy of Milan. He was already the ruler of the Netherlands, and married to Mary Tudor. In addition Philip would be a strong claimant to the throne of Portugal when Sebastian, the present king, died. Sebastian was killed in a battle against the Moors in 1578 but, before Philip could move towards the succession, Cardinal Prince Henry, Sebastian's great uncle, stepped in. However, aged, feeble, and almost insane, he died in 1580 and Philip's chance had come.

Of the five claimants to the vacant throne, only three had any real chance of succession. Philip's mother, Isabel, had been a princess of Portugal and his claim was a strong one. The other two candidates were Catharine, Duchess of Braganza, a granddaughter of a former king of Portugal, and Don Antonio, an illegitimate grandson of the same king. Catharine was bought off by Philip with the promise that her husband would be made King of Brazil if Philip became King of Portugal, a promise incidentally which was never fulfilled. Don Antonio moved quickly, proclaimed himself King, and occupied Lisbon. But the forces against him were too strong. In 1581 a Spanish army led by the Duke of Alva easily defeated the levies of Don Antonio, and Philip took the throne. We shall hear of Don Antonio again in the tangled story of the Armada campaign.

The throne of Portugal allied to the throne of Spain was a prospect that offered an almost unlimited source of world power and wealth. While the western voyages of discovery around the turn of the fifteenth century had brought Spain the wealth of the Americas, the eastern voyages in the same years had opened up the rich world of the East, which a handful of brave men had discovered and conquered for Portugal. And because in those days the fact of prior discovery was widely accepted as a right to monopoly of trade, Philip's future looked assured. His military position in Europe was unassailable and the fleet of Portugal added to that of Spain would be enough to guarantee exclusive trade development of the potential empires across the Atlantic and Indian Oceans.

The first crack in this picture of absolute power came with the failure of his marriage to Mary Tudor. Though she announced that she was pregnant a few months after the marriage, she was in fact barren and when she died in 1558 there was no heir of her body to continue her Catholic faith as the national religion. She was succeeded by her sister Elizabeth who, if she were to uphold Protestantism in a divided nation, would be forced by political necessity to become Philip's enemy.

In an attempt to repair the damage to his hopes and to prevent England becoming a hostile power on Spain's flank, Philip at once sent off a proposal of marriage to Elizabeth. It was an outrageous offer and would itself be a menace in the event of refusal. But the new Queen did not hesitate in turning it down.

The early years of Elizabeth's reign, while she was totally engaged in consolidating her position as a Protestant queen of a nation with a still sizeable Catholic minority, brought Philip a few years of precarious peace. But with the growth of Protestant power as Elizabeth established herself in England, and of Huguenot power as Henry of Navarre established himself in France, Philip found he was faced with an almost impossible situation. The revolt in the Netherlands, led by William the Silent, could be held with a Spanish army of occupation, though at a considerable cost; but when Elizabeth, after William's assassination, stepped into the Dutch revolt with a contribution of 6,000 fighting men, and at the same time actively supported the Huguenot cause in France with cash subsidies, Philip was inevitably committed to a long struggle in which he could not emerge victorious except by the conquest of France and England. Neither side was as yet ready for an all-out war; the conflict between them was conducted on the principle of reprisals, a doctrine under which local acts of war could be countered by equivalent acts of retribution without committing the nations involved to the full rigours of active warfare.

In Philip's predicament there was only one solution, which was to renounce his inheritance of the Low Countries and so remove that crippling drain on the Spanish economy. Without a costly army of occupation to hold down the Dutch revolt, and with the considerable naval reinforcement which Portugal had provided, he would have enough naval and military power to face the prospect of a war against England with some confidence. It was a solution put forward by some of his advisers but it was not within Philip's make-up even to consider it. His education, his natural disposition, his pride as the ruler of an immense empire, made it impossible for him to take such a course. It was also morally impossible for him to believe that he could be in the wrong in enforcing Catholicism on each and every one of his subjects. Family pride, too, was a considerable element in his decision to hold on to every corner of his empire,

Spanish troops leaving Maastricht in the Netherlands. Under the leadership of Alexander Farnese, Duke of Parma, they had the reputation of being the finest soldiers in Europe. An illustration from Baron Michael Eytzinger's De Leone Belgico *of 1583.*

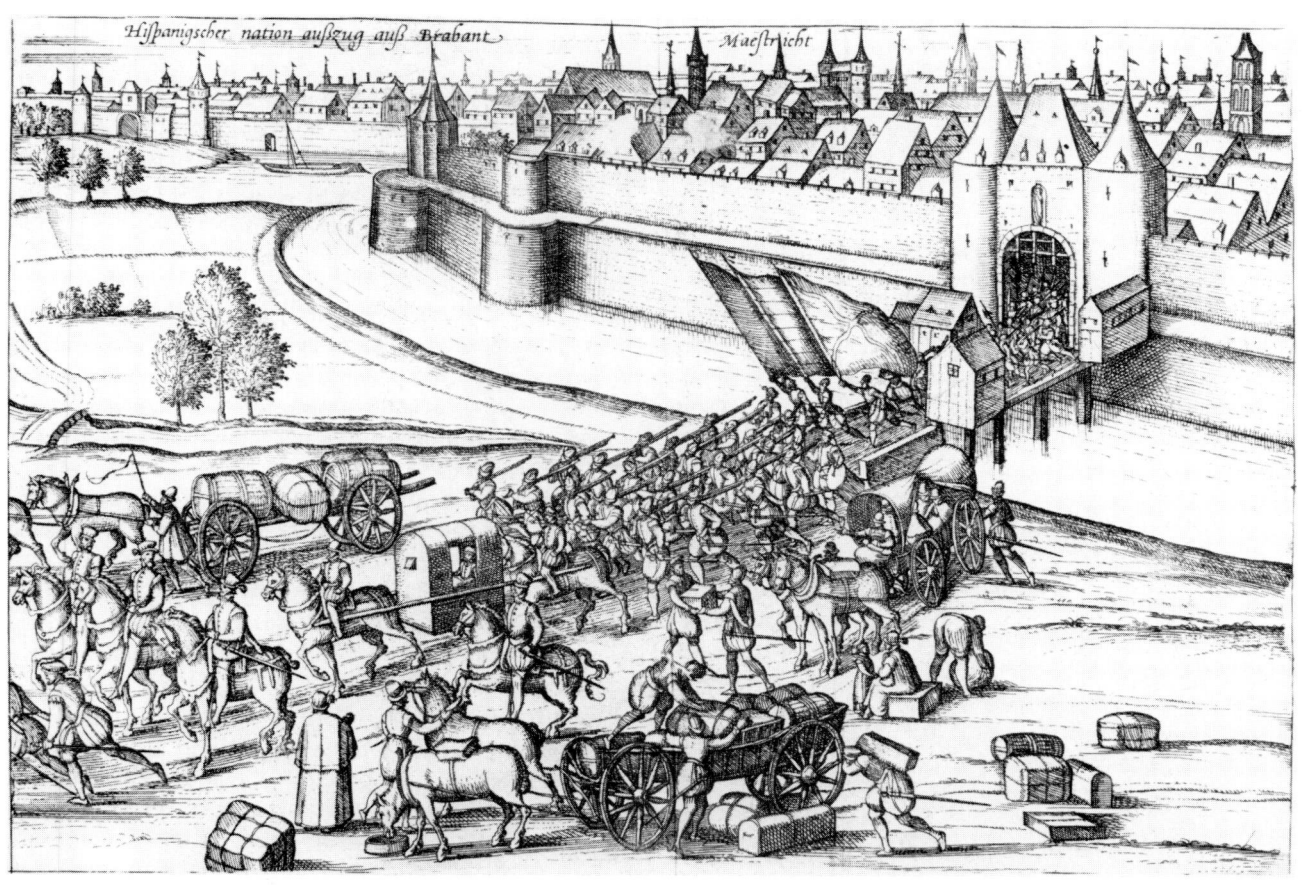

and in this respect he was immensely proud, even to the point of arrogance. These influences finally forced him into a conflict which quickly assumed the character of a struggle between Roman Catholicism and Protestantism, with Philip as the champion of the Holy Church. It was a part he gloried in playing, and if to play it he was forced also to become a persecutor in the name of Roman Catholicism, both in and out of Spain, so be it. Already his religious persecutions had fuelled the obstinacy of the Dutch revolt; he had continually infuriated the English and driven them into yet more reprisals; and he had drained the Spanish Treasury in suppressing the revolt of the Moors. But the evident failure of his policies could not shake his belief in their essential excellence. Whatever he did was done for the service of God, and success or failure depended on the inscrutable will of the Almighty and not on himself. This was ever his guiding conviction. It was a comforting belief and undoubtedly he fostered it to the full. It was true that he was ready to make use of assassination for his political purposes, but he accepted without question the advice of his lawyers and advisers that as the King he was indeed the embodied State and had the right and duty to act individually for the public good. It was beyond belief that his European policy might in the end bring Spain to ruin.

But there was another side to Philip. Although many historians have painted him in the colours almost of a monk, picturing him endlessly at work in his cell-like study in his Palace of the Escurial with its private entrance into the chapel next door, Philip also had the appetites of a man. He is said to have been extremely licentious as a young man and later lived for years with Maria de Orsario as his mistress, though he was probably a good deal less immoral in this respect than most other European kings and princes of the period, including his own father. And he had the ambitions of a man with the world at his feet, a burning desire to bring into reality that dream of world power to which the circumstances of his inheritance pointed. If a part of the driving force could be attributed to God, the rest of it came unquestionably from Philip the man.

In spite of the mounting tension as the struggle between Protestantism and Roman Catholicism sharpened, there remained one small gleam of light for Philip. Elizabeth was still unmarried and was of an age that made it unlikely that she could produce a direct heir to her throne. Unless by some miracle she did, the next heir was Mary Stuart, Queen of Scotland. She had been brought up in France as a Catholic and was still a Catholic in spite of a somewhat unsavoury reputation following her tempestuous marriages with Henry Darnley and James Bothwell. If Elizabeth were to die and Mary to succeed, England might yet return to Catholicism and solve one of Philip's problems by outflanking France to the north.

It was perhaps a tenuous possibility, and it brought with it an uncomfortable consideration. Even if Elizabeth continued with her growing aggression in the waters which Philip considered his own—and Philip had no doubts that she would—would it be wise for him to attempt an active invasion of England while Mary Stuart, and the hopes he had vested in her, was still alive? These thoughts placed a political and personal constraint on him which he could not totally ignore.

France was less worried by the possibility of an alliance between England and Spain. Mary had been brought up since childhood in the French Court and had married Francis, son of Henry II and Catherine de Medici, to become Queen of France. She would hardly desert a country with which she had been so closely associated. It was

Portrait of Philip II of Spain and Mary I of England, attributed to Hans Eworth. Their marriage in 1554 was arranged by Charles V with the object of isolating France and ensuring Spanish control of the English Channel.

Philip II and his family, painted in 1585. His wife, Anne, stands with their son, Philip, and one of her sisters. Anne was the daughter of Maximilian II, King of Hungary. She was Philip's fourth wife.

true that many Frenchmen found it difficult to forgive the part Mary had played in the beheading of Pierre de Chastelard, one of the French nobles who had accompanied her from France to Scotland after the death of her first husband. His crime was to have been twice discovered in her bedroom at night and his execution was hurried through at Mary's instigation in case he had any embarrassing comments to make. But as Queen of England her value to France would be much too great to allow such an incident to rankle, and all Mary's past ties would surely make it impossible for her to throw in her lot with France's current enemy, Spain. It is ironic that, in fact, Philip already had a letter from Mary Stuart in his possession pledging her alliance to Spain when she succeeded Elizabeth on the throne of England.

In any case, France was engulfed in civil war, the War of the Three Henries. Henry of Valois, the present king, had no direct heir and was trying to hold a precarious position in the fighting between Henry of Guise, the champion of Roman Catholicism and heavily subsidized by Philip, and Henry of Navarre, the champion of the Huguenots and equally heavily subsidized by Elizabeth. Both had claims to the throne when Valois died, and the results of the fighting would decide which Henry would succeed. The ifs and buts of Mary Stuart's possible accession to the English throne held a secondary place in French calculations in comparison with the swaying fortunes of the civil war.

Shorn of its political and religious shades, the crux of all Philip's plans and dreams rested in the control of the English Channel. In the burgeoning of seaborne trade throughout the sixteenth century it was the essential highway for the ships of northern Europe to the oceans of the world and their promise of riches. In those days of small ships with their unwieldy hull design and inefficient sail plan, the alternative route to the west around the north of Scotland was, if not quite an economic impossibility, at least a tremendous burden, adding some 1,500 miles to their trading voyages through waters still largely unknown and uncharted. If Philip could control the Channel with his fleet, he could shut out northern Europe from that trade across the oceans. And in any war against England he could get nowhere until his ships could not only pass freely through the Channel to support and succour his invasion army but also deny its use to the English fleet.

Just as it was important for Philip to take control of the Channel it was equally important for the countries along its shores that he should not do so. As a defence against a Spanish attempt at invasion, the Channel was vital to England. It was vital, too, to France, for with the Channel in Spanish hands there could be no security for her future independence as a nation. Spanish power would surround her in the south, the east, and the north. And it was even more vital to the Dutch. As the great sea carriers of Europe, the English Channel was for them an essential highway for the trade that produced their wealth. Without its free use by their merchant ships, their long fight against the Spanish occupation of their territories could no longer be financially maintained.

As the years passed and the tension between Spain and England mounted, the other countries of Europe watched with growing anxiety. Spanish sea power was dominant on the oceans and her armies were recognized as the finest fighting force in Europe. And England's reputation at sea rested not on battles fought and won but on the small scale reprisals against Spain which, though generally successful, were little short of adventurous piracy. The mettle of her army was unknown, but its leadership was suspect if the example of those 6,000 fighting men sent by Elizabeth to assist the Dutch in their revolt was a true guide. Elizabeth's choice of the Earl of Leicester to lead the army had been a disaster, and the Dutch resented the pomp and luxury with which he surrounded himself and his reluctance to commit his army to active warfare. In the face of the generally perceived odds, the Protestant cause did not appear yet to stand on very solid ground.

And as far away as Rome the new Pope, Sixtus V, whose concern was of course to ensure the universality of the Catholic faith, expressed his interest with a promise to Philip of a million gold ducats to be paid when the first Spanish soldiers landed on the shores of England. Implicit in his promise was an element of punishment of Elizabeth, already declared a heretic by Papal Bull for continuing to uphold the apostasy of her father.

NOT LONGE TIME SINCE I SAWE A COWE.
DID FLAVNDERS REPRESENTE
VPON WHOSE BACKE KINGE PHILLIP RODE
AS BEING MALECONTNT.

THE QVEENE OF ENGLAND GIVING HAY
WHEARE ON THE COW DID FEEDE.
AS ONE THAT WAS HER GREATEST HELPE.
IN HER DISTRESSE AND NEEDE.

THE PRINCE OF ORANGE MILKT THE CO
AND MADE HIS PVRSE THE PAYLE.
THE COW DID SHYT IN MONSIEVRS HAND
WHILE HE DID HOLD HER TAYLE.

'The Milch Cow', a political cartoon inspired by a Paris pantomime in 1579. The cow represents Flanders; Philip
of Spain sits on its back and beats it; Elizabeth of England stands at its head and feeds it with troops and subsidies;
William of Orange sits beneath it and drinks its milk; and the Duke of Anjou (later Henry III of France), in
his office of Defender of the Liberties of the Netherlands, holds its tail.

Opposite: Henry III of France attending the first assembly of the Holy Spirit, a religious order which he founded.
The Duc de Nevers is taking the oath, while in the back row, left, stand three of the King's 'mignons'.

2 San Juan De Ulloa 1568

Trade between England and Spain was well established in the sixteenth century, dating back at least 200 years, and was enshrined in a number of commercial treaties of which the most recent had been signed in 1495 by Henry VII of England and Philip of Burgundy, father of Charles, King of Spain and Holy Roman Emperor. These commercial treaties were based on the freedom of the high seas and reciprocal rights to trade freely in each other's ports. The ratification of the 1495 treaty extended to each side's heirs and successors, and so were binding on both Elizabeth and Philip.

Since the signature of that treaty, knowledge of the world had been greatly expanded through the Spanish and Portuguese voyages of discovery. To apportion the discoveries the then Pope had been persuaded to draw a meridional line through the Atlantic Ocean, allotting to Spain all discoveries to the west of it and to Portugal all discoveries to the east, and had announced monopoly trading rights in these discoveries by a Papal Bull. The other countries of Europe had been less fortunate in their attempts to discover sea routes to the new lands, particularly England, whose voyages to reach the riches of the East by new passages to the Pacific Ocean to the north-east and north-west had been blocked by polar ice.

A Papal Bull was predictably disregarded in Protestant England and the Netherlands; in Catholic France the urgencies of trade expansion easily outweighed any religious allegiance to so arbitrary a ruling from Rome. In the spirit of the times and the restless urge to expand and grow richer, particularly in Tudor England, it was expected that it might well prove necessary to use force to dispute the Papal Bull.

It was the Portuguese who first felt the force of the English reply. Although the early English voyages to the Guinea coast were resisted by Portuguese warships, the length of the African coastline was too extended to be adequately guarded and there were many local African chiefs anxious to welcome newcomers with their cargoes of trade goods. From these Guinea voyages the English merchants first learned of the large profits to be made from the shipment and sale of African negroes to the Spanish colonists in the West Indies.

This venture took root in the business brain of John Hawkins. He was an experienced seaman with several successful trading voyages to Spain and the Canary Islands to his credit and at the same time was something of a merchant prince in the City of London. He had married the daughter of Benjamin Gonson, Treasurer of Elizabeth's navy, and through his father-in-law had some access to the Court in relation to its naval affairs. To make the most of the new opportunity, he planned a series of triangular voyages, the first leg to the Guinea coast with trade goods for sale, the second to

View of a shipbuilder's yard in Seville. During the sixteenth century Seville was one of the busiest ports in Spain and an important centre for shipbuilding.

the West Indies to sell his human cargo and invest the proceeds in hides, sugar, and other West Indian produce, and the third leg of the triangle home to realize the profit. He relied on the terms of the commercial treaty of 1495 for the freedom to trade in West Indian ports, on the grounds that a Spanish port was a Spanish port whether in Spain herself or in her colonies.

His first venture with three small ships, all privately owned, set out in 1557. It proved a considerable commercial success even though it ended on a sour note. After selling most of the negroes in Hispaniola, Hawkins had to charter two additional ships to carry his accumulated cargoes home and, as an earnest of the legality of his trade, directed them to Spain for the sale of their cargoes on his account. On their arrival, both cargoes were seized by the Spanish authorities and confiscated on the pretext that the voyage was piratical. Although their loss was assessed by Hawkins at 40,000 ducats, the profits on the three ships which did return to England handsomely outweighed the loss.

Hawkins's third triangular voyage ended in disaster at San Juan de Ulloa in the West Indies, but it was a disaster which, though perhaps indirectly, had a considerable bearing on the failure of Philip's 'Enterprise of England' when he launched it twenty years later. Two royal ships, the *Jesus of Lubeck* of 600 tons and the *Minion* of 200 tons, were included in the squadron on a profit-sharing basis, and Hawkins and his city friends provided three more, one of them the *Judith* commanded by a young relative of Hawkins named Francis Drake, hitherto unknown. The voyage was prepared in secrecy, but when a rumour of its intended destination leaked out, the Spanish ambassador protested vigorously to Lord Burghley, Elizabeth's Secretary of State and Lord High Treasurer, only to be assured that it was a trading venture to the east and would not be visiting Spanish colonies in the west.

It sailed in 1568, sold its negroes on the Spanish Main, admittedly with some strong-arm persuasion of the Spanish local authorities to permit their sale, and put in to the small port of San Juan de Ulloa to take on board fresh water and provisions for the voyage home. The safety of the ships was guaranteed by the captain of the port. A Spanish squadron arrived outside the port next day and although Hawkins was strong enough to deny it entry, he allowed it to enter under another guarantee from the Spanish admiral that no harm to his ships would occur. At a dinner on board the *Jesus of Lubeck* given by Hawkins for the Spanish admiral and his principal officers, one of the guests was discovered to have a dagger concealed in his sleeve. While he was being disarmed the admiral gave a signal and the English ships were violently attacked. The *Minion* and *Judith* both managed to escape but the *Jesus of Lubeck* and two smaller ships were destroyed. There was a considerable loss of life on both sides.

Hawkins himself escaped in the *Minion* and Drake in his own ship, the *Judith*. When the *Minion* reached England with news of the disaster, the whole country was joined in fury at the treachery of the Spaniards and demanded war against Spain. But neither Elizabeth nor Philip was ready for so final a sanction and the wound was allowed to fester in a series of reprisals that still further stirred up the bad blood between the two nations.

San Juan de Ulloa proved to be a black day for any Spanish intentions for an eventual conquest of England. An immediate English response was the capture of some Spanish treasure ships in the Atlantic in retribution for the attack. More far-reaching in its effect was Drake's determination to exact vengeance, and his marauding voyages

Sir John Hawkins, painted three years after the Armada battles. As well as a fighting admiral he was Treasurer of the Navy Board and was largely concerned with all the administrative work of building and repairing ships and keeping them supplied.

to the Spanish Main and Panama, and later into the Pacific, forced Spain to equip and maintain naval forces to guard the collection of treasure in those waters for eventual transport to Spain in the yearly *flotas*. It was an annual expenditure which Spain could ill afford and it starved Philip of the financial means adequately to support the Duke of Parma and his army in the Netherlands. And this, in its turn, prevented the clear-cut victory over the Dutch resistance which was a vital element if the campaign against England was to have any real chance of success.

The experience of San Juan de Ulloa took Hawkins in a different direction, one which was to have a direct influence on the tactical battles of the Spanish Armada itself. The loss of Elizabeth's *Jesus of Lubeck* required an explanation at Court, and with his seaman's mind Hawkins looked first at the design of the ship to explain her loss, and then at that of the *Minion* and *Judith* to explain their escape. He was convinced that the high forecastle built up over the bow of the former presented too great a surface to the wind for efficient sailing and that the lower freeboard of the smaller *Minion* and *Judith* contributed to their escape. With the naval influence of his father-in-

A Spanish drawing of 1590 of the fortified island of San Juan de Ulloa, the scene of Hawkins's disaster of 1568. Ships using the port were secured to heavy rings set in the stonework of the wharf, with their anchors laid out astern.

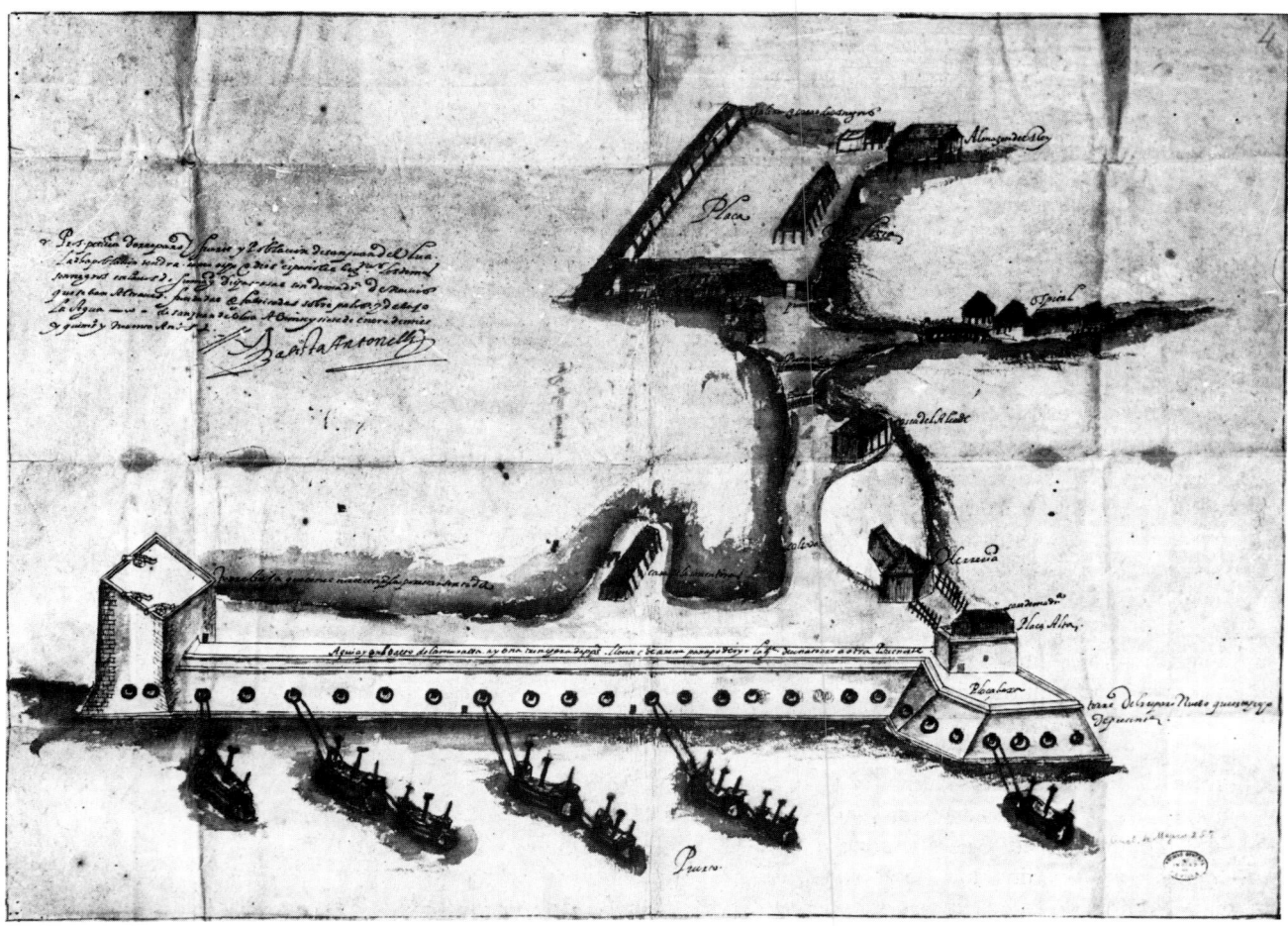

law, and probably with the aid of Matthew Baker, principal shipwright in the naval yard at Woolwich, Hawkins was given the opportunity to try his new design with two small ships, the *Bull* and the *Tiger*, which were brought into the yard in 1570 for rebuilding.

The old design, common throughout the navies of Europe, was based on the Spanish and Portuguese carrack, with the high castles at each end designed to provide defensive fire on any attempt by an enemy to capture the ship by boarding across the low waist-deck. What Hawkins wanted was a flush-decked ship built lower in the water than a carrack and with a cut-down forecastle moved aft from the bow. At the same time he wanted an increase in the length-to-beam ratio to provide a better hull shape, and a square stern in place of a rounded one. On the completion of work on the *Bull* and the *Tiger* it was apparent that his design had made a great improvement, with an increase of about one knot in speed and an ability to lie one compass point closer to the wind when sailing close-hauled. With the ship lying lower in the water, she also presented a smaller target to enemy gunners. The improvements were decisive, and all new naval ships were now built to the new design, as were the older ships brought in for rebuilding.

At the same time there was a simplification in the types of guns mounted, the work of Sir William Wynter. In the navy of Henry VIII there had been no less than twenty-two different naval guns; Wynter now reduced them to five. The largest was the demi-cannon, a heavy anti-ship gun firing a 30-lb. ball to a distance of 1,700 yards. The two other anti-ship guns mounted were culverins and demi-culverins, long-barrelled guns throwing a 17-lb. or 9-lb. shot with reasonable accuracy to a range of about 2,700 yards. Anti-personnel guns, mounted to repel boarders, were periers and petards, firing stone balls and case-shot with a good rate of fire. Another of Wynter's improvements was the substitution of brass in place of iron in the casting of guns to provide greater strength, weight for weight, and less chance of a burst when the powder charge was ignited. Great progress was made in replacing the iron guns, and in a report of 1582 it was recorded that of the total of 682 demi-cannons and culverins mounted in naval ships, only fifty were still of iron.

The English gunfounders were much admired throughout Europe and their guns held in high repute because of their accuracy, particularly the long-barrelled culverins. After the death of Santa Cruz early in 1588, his successor, the Duke of Medina Sidonia, made desperate appeals to Philip for more guns, particularly cannons, demi-cannons, and culverins for the Armada's galleons. Philip gave orders for more to be cast at the arsenals at Madrid and Lisbon, but few gunfounders in those days were experienced in the art of casting big guns and of those few most lived in England. Some of the shortage was made good by the purchase of guns from foreign ships in Spanish ports, but even when the Armada finally sailed later that year the problem had not yet been fully solved. Almost all the main battery guns were short-barrelled with no more than half the range of the English guns.

There was one other difference between the English navy and those of the rest of Europe. During Elizabeth's reign her navy adopted the strategic concept that more advantage was to be gained in carrying the fight to the enemy at sea than to wait and fight him defensively when he attacked. English naval leaders from the Lord High Admiral, Howard of Effingham, downwards, and particularly John Hawkins and Francis Drake, were firm believers in this school of thought. With the new design of ship and the new guns, the advantage of their belligerence was confirmed, and their confidence and skill in attack was to cost Philip his hoped-for victory.

It was England's good fortune that Philip's 'Enterprise of England' came when it did. The art of naval warfare was emerging from its first great period of change, from the formalized, almost mechanical, galley warfare, which had been the method of fighting at sea from the earliest days, to a new period of sailing ships of war which had nothing in common with their predecessors. The galley had of necessity to be a long ship with a narrow beam and a low freeboard so that its rowers could propel it through the water, and because of this it was unstable in any but calm seas. It was a warship of short endurance because its multitude of crew—soldiers, sailors, rowers, cooks, artisans, etc.—occupied so much space that there was little left for the stowage of food, water, ammunition, and other essentials. And because the rowers had to sit on benches amidships galleys had to have their guns mounted on the foredeck so that they were ahead-firing ships. Individual galleys and fleets of galleys were commanded by soldiers and their tactical handling in battle resembled more a military action on land than a naval action at sea. The one great asset enjoyed by the galley in battle was the free movement independent of the wind which its rowers gave it.

For centuries Spain had been a naval power in the Mediterranean and only during the last fifty or so years had she had to adapt to the very different fighting conditions of the Atlantic. Naval war in the Mediterranean was still galley warfare, and even as the Armada sailed in 1588, Philip was maintaining a fleet of more than 100 galleys in his Mediterranean ports. The development of the galleasse, in which the rowers' benches were decked over to provide a platform for broadside guns, was an attempt to combine the qualities of the galley and the sailing warship. She was fitted with masts and sails and the typical castles forward and aft, and was designed to use her rowers in battle only when she might require independence of the wind. Inevitably the galleasses had to be very large ships to accommodate crews, including the rowers, of more than seven hundred. Although their use in breaking up the Turkish attack formation at Lepanto was decisive in the outcome of that battle, they were still no more than a hybrid, with little value in the turbulent waters outside the Mediterranean. Philip included a squadron of four of them in his Armada fleet and they were to have very little influence on the outcome of individual actions.

Opposite: The new English warship design evolved by Hawkins, drawn by Matthew Baker in about 1585. This is the earliest technical drawing of an English ship to survive. It shows the flush deck and lower fore- and aftercastles of the new design. The cod below the ship indicates the desired shape of the ship's bottom.

Right: A diagram comparing the new design with the old. The more streamlined shape of the new warships brought considerable advantages in speed and sailing quality.

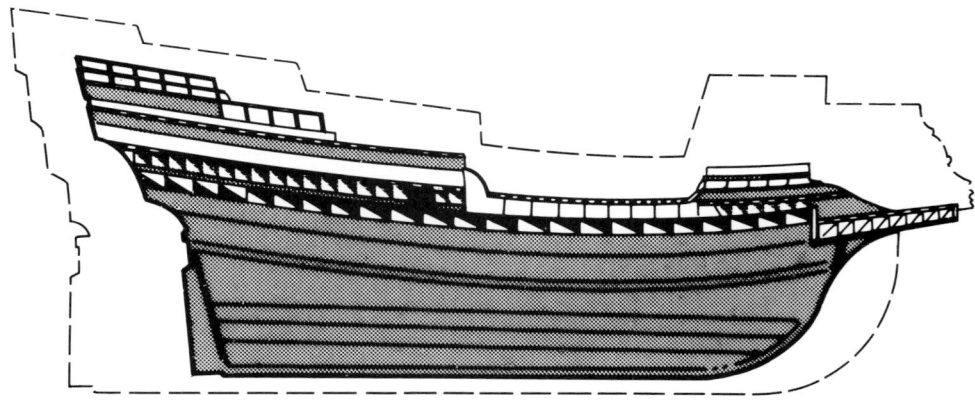

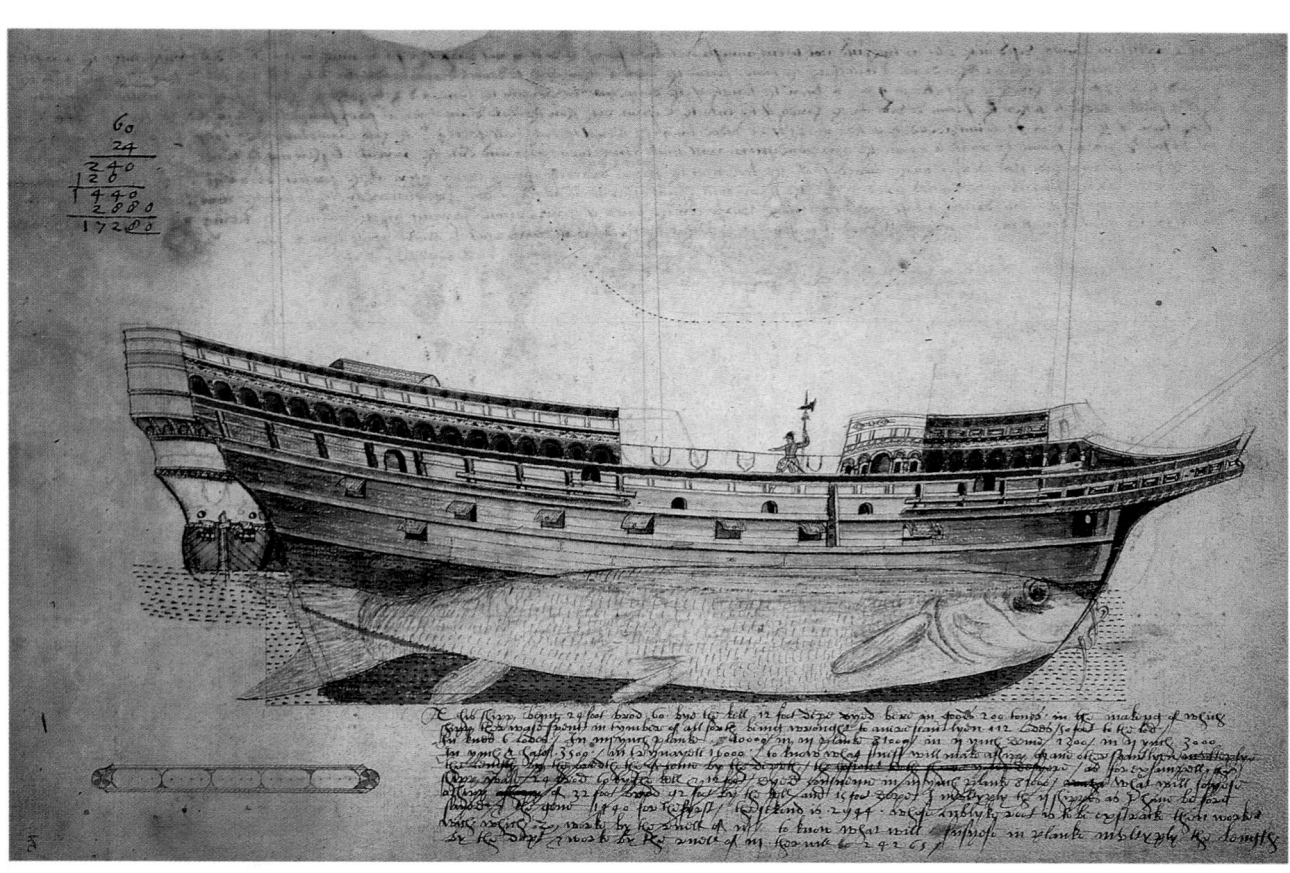

One glaring weakness in Philip's sailing warships was the failure of the crews to adapt to the new conditions. The galley tradition was so strongly entrenched in their naval philosophy that it became impossible to throw it off when the warship under sails took over from the warship under oars as the principal fighting ship in waters beyond the Mediterranean. The internal organization of the Spanish sailing warship was the same as that of the galley, totally military and not unlike the organization of a fortress on land. The ship's company was divided into three distinct classes, soldiers, gunners, and sailors, with the soldiers in overall command. The naval captain of the sailing warship corresponded to the English rank of master and he was only responsible for the ship's navigation. He came under the direct command of the military captain in every other aspect of the ship's work. The sailors who worked the ship were always at the bottom of the pile. Sir Richard Hawkins wrote of them: 'The mariners are but as slaves to the rest, to moil and toil day and night . . . and not suffered to sleep or harbour themselves under the decks.' It was an organization that may have worked reasonably well in a short endurance warship such as the galley, but in a long endurance warship such as the galleon it was a certain recipe for disaster.

Apart from his Mediterranean galley fleet, Philip's forces in the Atlantic were very thinly spread. The Indian Guard, a naval force of galleons and smaller ships, mainly caravels, was permanently stationed in the West Indies to protect the trade and provide an escort for the *flota* of treasure ships on their voyages across the Atlantic to Spain. Most of their cost was covered by a special levy on the merchants engaged in this trade, and their withdrawal for other purposes would be a clear breach of faith with the merchants. Apart from the Indian Guard and the Mediterranean galleys and galleasses, there were few other ships in Spain that could be counted as warships.

The picture changed radically in 1581 when Philip's bid for the throne of Portugal was successful. The Portuguese navy was built around twelve good galleons, though one of these was lost in the action to capture Lisbon and expel Don Antonio. Later that year Philip ordered nine new galleons to be built in the Biscay yards, and more orders for galleons followed, as Philip's thoughts increasingly concentrated on the need to settle his differences with England. There were other sources of reinforcement; some of the other Mediterranean states had galleons in their navies and the Pope was always more than ready to put whatever pressure he could on them to contribute their ships to what, in his opinion, was a war against heresy.

By 1586 Philip had collected a considerable fleet. Spain was by then in a virtual state of war with England after Drake's Indies voyage of 1585–6 (see pp. 37–43), though Philip and Elizabeth were both still unready to put the decision to the touch. Philip's reluctance lay not only in his hope of yet more promises of aid from the Mediterranean to swell his fleet but also in the fact that Mary Stuart was still alive and still the heir to Elizabeth's throne, even though she was a prisoner in England. Her accession would solve all his difficulties with England without a blow having to be struck. Elizabeth's reluctance was almost entirely financial; the drain on national finance of her aid to the Netherlands and to Navarre was still considerable and though she never lacked courage, she was not the sort of person to take risks unless and until there was no other course of action. While Philip remained quiet, she would do the same. Her caution, which at times amounted almost to indecision, was backed up by William Cecil, Lord Burghley, one of the staunchest bulwarks of English Protestantism.

While still waiting for the last few of the promised galleons to arrive, Philip began to grow impatient and wrote almost daily to the Marquis of Santa Cruz, now Captain General of the Ocean Sea, urging him to new endeavours to get the Armada to sea. But Santa Cruz, the hero of so many battles, was getting old and, though none could ever doubt his courage, was overwhelmed by the difficulties facing a Spanish fleet in so great an enterprise as an invasion of England. However, when Philip, buoyed up by promises of further reinforcements and the offer from the Pope of his million gold ducats, sent Santa Cruz a list of the ships which would be available to him, the old marquis began to express a cautious confidence that the 'Enterprise of England' might not prove so forlorn an adventure as earlier it had looked to be.

English shipwrights of the sixteenth century, the frontispiece to Matthew Baker's treatise on shipwrightery. Baker was principal shipwright in the naval dockyard at Woolwich.

The Jesus of Lubeck, one of the Queen's ships which was lost at San Juan de Ulloa. She was of the old well-deck design, with a large protruding forecastle and high aftercastle.

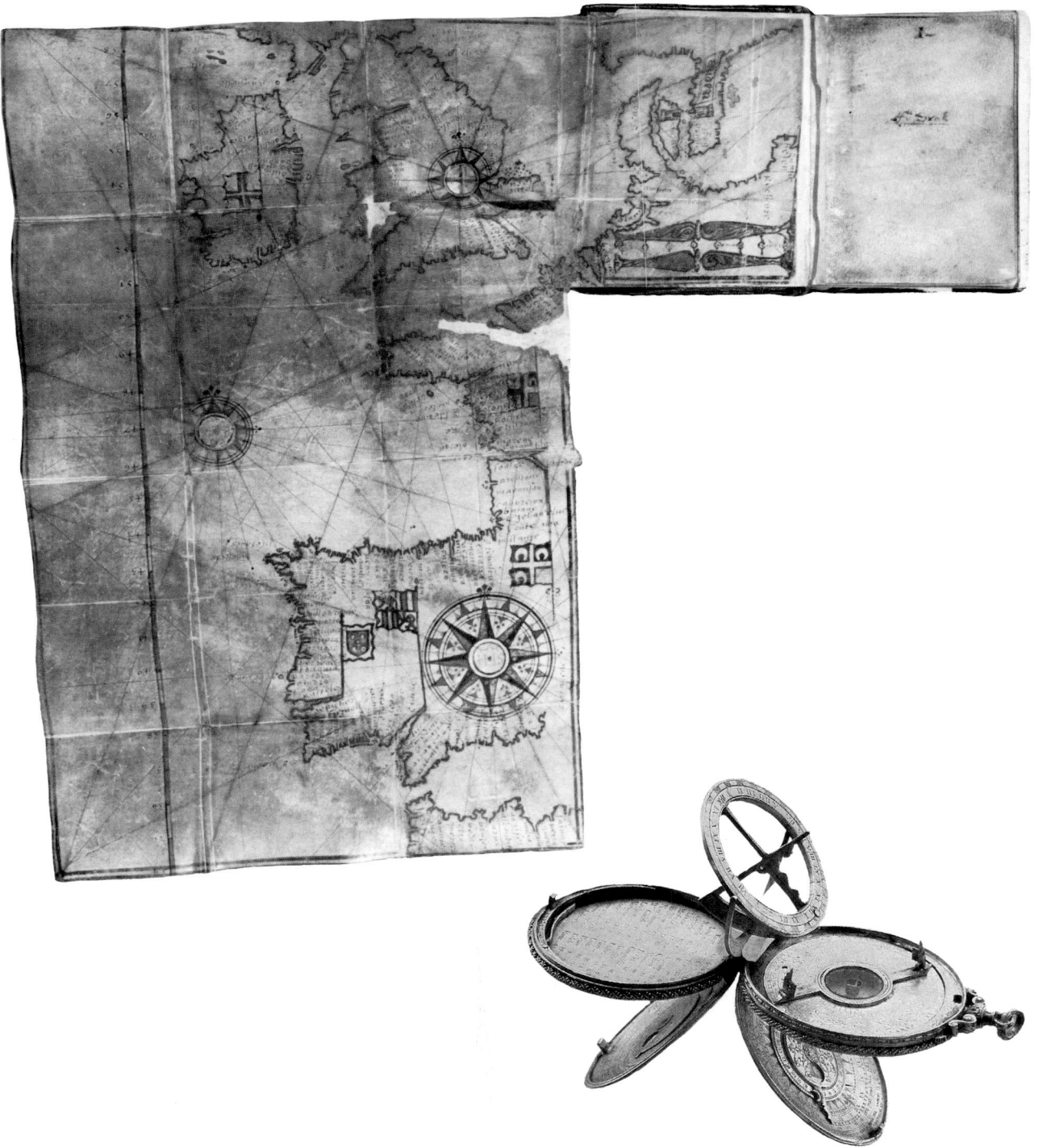

3 The Indies Voyage 1585~6

It is impossible in the tangled and varying state of relations between England and Spain during the early years of the 1580s to point to any one particular moment or episode as the start of formal war between the two nations. Drake's expedition of 1585–6 to the West Indies has been generally accepted as the *de facto* starting point, which is probably accurate enough, though it was followed by no official declaration of war and the warlike operations which succeeded it only differed in degree from what had gone before. It suited the policies of both Elizabeth and Philip to retain the informalities of general reprisal even though both recognized that full hostilities were inevitable unless Philip withdrew his much publicized threats of invasion.

During these years of the early 1580s there had been a considerable acceleration of shipbuilding in England. It represented the Tudor urge to push out into a wider trading world than that of Europe alone and a willingness to fight for the right to trade if such extreme measures were necessary. All merchant ships of any size in those days went armed, very much on naval lines, and were also recognized as potential and valuable additions to the war fleets in time of battle. In England's case, though Elizabeth could muster twenty-five or so royal ships which constituted her navy, there would be no difficulty, with armed merchant ships to back them up, of raising a fleet of over a hundred ships to fight her battles.

Nor would there be any problem in finding men to work the ships. English warships were manned partly by volunteers and partly by pressed men. Most of the pressed men were trained to the sea, and came either from merchant ships, or from the ports and waterways. As in all other navies, the discipline they faced on board was fierce and arbitrary though perhaps no more so than the hardships faced by the labouring classes ashore.

Two years before the Armada sailed from Spain the pay of the English seaman was raised from 6s. 8d. to 10s. per lunar month (thirteen months to the year), out of which he was expected to provide his own clothing. Some sort of uniform had evolved for work at sea, and most Elizabethan seamen wore a canvas shift tucked into very wide-cut canvas breeches to form a kind of apron in front, known as galligaskins or petticoat-trousers. Almost invariably seamen painted them with tar as a form of waterproofing for work on deck and on the yards, and this earned them the name of 'tarry-breeks', probably the origin of the later nickname Jack Tar used to describe a sailor. Seamen raised specifically for the Armada campaign in 1587 and 1588 received a bonus of a blue coat given by the Queen, perhaps one of the earliest indications that blue was to become the favoured colour for naval uniform throughout the world.

Opposite, above: Sir Francis Drake's pocket map of the English, French and Spanish coasts. In spite of the compass rose and plumb lines the map would have been of little use for navigation, but it gave him a rough outline from which to plan his operations.

Below: Drake's compass and dial, a small combined navigational instrument carried by the great sea commander.

Life at sea was far from easy. Victuals, invariably an administrative headache through the vagaries of supply in sailing ships dependent on wind and weather, consisted of salt beef and salt pork stored in casks filled with brine, dried fish, pease, hard-baked biscuit, and cheese, with a daily allowance of one gallon of beer. Inevitably some of the provisions went bad or were attacked by weevils but frequently even the bad food had to be issued because there was nothing else on board to take its place. It was in any case a diet almost guaranteed to engender scurvy, one of the two great killer diseases to which seamen were prone. The other was typhus, spread by lice which flourished in the dirty and fetid atmosphere below decks and encouraged by the fact that it was rare for a seaman in those days to have a change of clothing. All navies and merchant navies of the period suffered from these two diseases, and many more men died from them than were ever killed in battle. Yet with all the dangers and hardships which faced the contemporary seaman, there was at that time a spirit of adventure which called men to the sea, and it was rare in those days for a ship to be held back from sailing because of a lack of men to man her.

The surge in English shipbuilding had not gone unnoticed in Spain. As long ago as 1581 Don Bernardino de Mendoza, the Spanish ambassador in London, had warned Philip of the growing danger to Spanish aspirations. 'They are building ships without cessation,' he wrote, 'and they are thus making themselves masters at sea. All this swells their pride as they see their country with such multitudes of ships and they think that therefore they are unassailable by any prince on earth.'

Philip no doubt absorbed Mendoza's warning but by 1585 he was much more confident than he had been earlier. He made no secret of his plans for the conquest of England and exaggerated estimates of the huge fleet he was collecting for this enterprise were current throughout Europe. It was in these circumstances that Drake, who had the ear of the Queen, proposed an attack on Spain's oceanic trade and her American colonies, aimed at reducing Philip's naval strength. His choice of the American colonies was designed deliberately to appeal to the merchants, who would finance the expedition, and to Elizabeth, who would stand to profit from the adventure through the royal ships she would contribute to the squadron.

Elizabeth, however, proved difficult to convince. Drake had proposed a covert operation under the flag of Don Antonio, the Portuguese pretender, and if that proved impossible, an open expedition as a general reprisal against the ships of Spain. He had the enthusiastic backing of Robert Dudley, Earl of Leicester, the Queen's favourite, of Francis Walsingham, the principal Secretary of State, and of Hawkins, now Treasurer of the Navy. Elizabeth set conditions for her approval. If France, which since 1580 had embraced Don Antonio's cause, was prepared to co-operate with England in the expedition Elizabeth would issue the necessary Letters of general reprisal; without France at her side she could not consent. In fact, the French, with their southern and eastern frontiers both wide open to Spanish military forces, were so unlikely to agree that the project was never even discussed with them.

Surprisingly, it was Philip of Spain who solved this problem for Elizabeth and for Drake and his backers. After a series of bad harvests in Spain he invited English corn ships to Spanish harbours, with guarantees of immunity from any restrictions, religious or otherwise, on the sale of their cargoes. The moment they arrived he declared an embargo on all English shipping, seized the vessels, and arrested their crews. Only one English ship, the *Primrose*, escaped. While discharging her cargo at Bilbao she had

A sixteenth-century map of the Thames estuary with eighteen ships lying in the River Medway below Rochester and Chatham. Most of the new warships built for the navy to the design of Hawkins and Baker were constructed in the dockyard at Chatham.

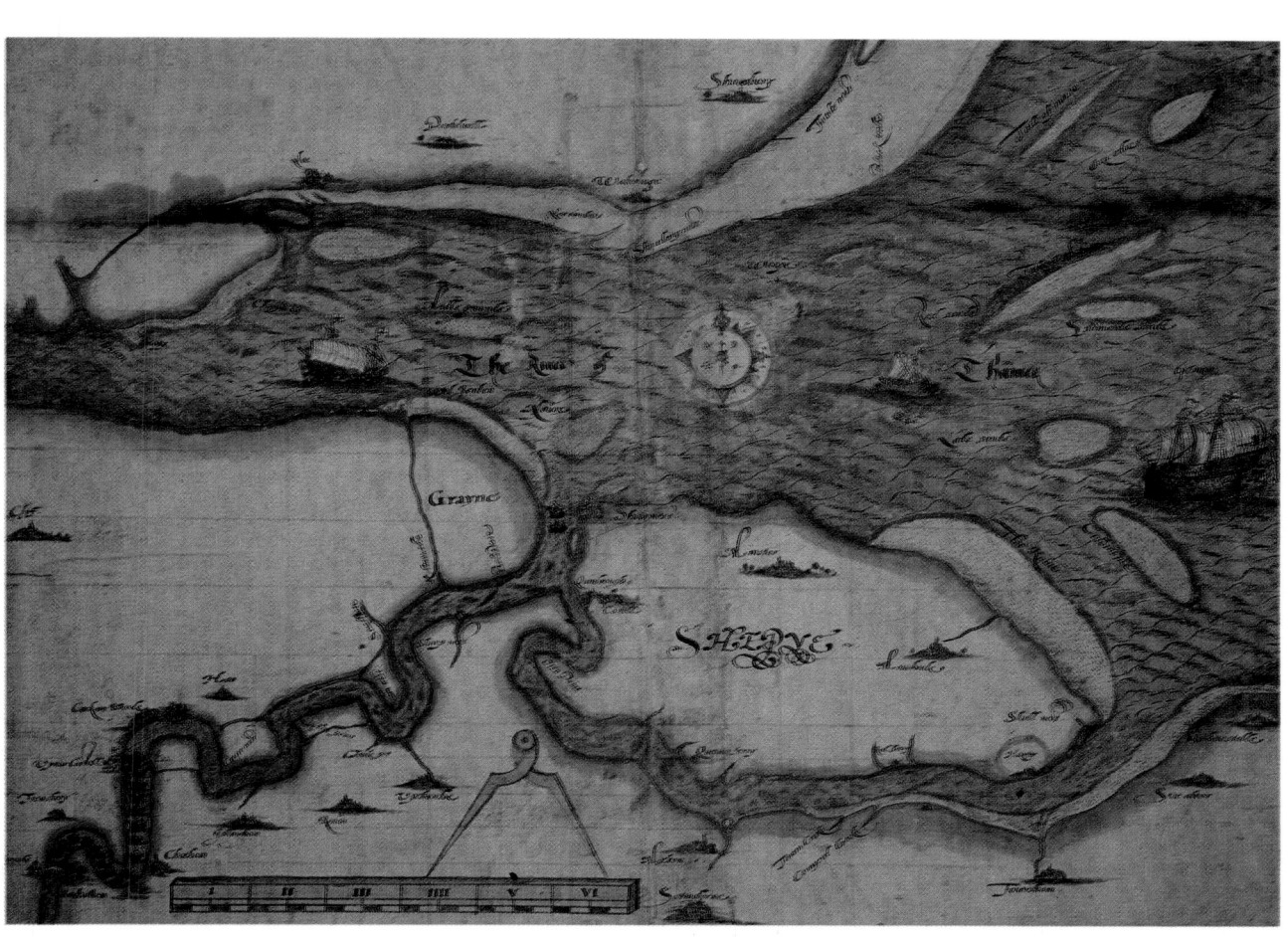

A chart of Drake's Indies voyage, traced on a contemporary map of the Atlantic.

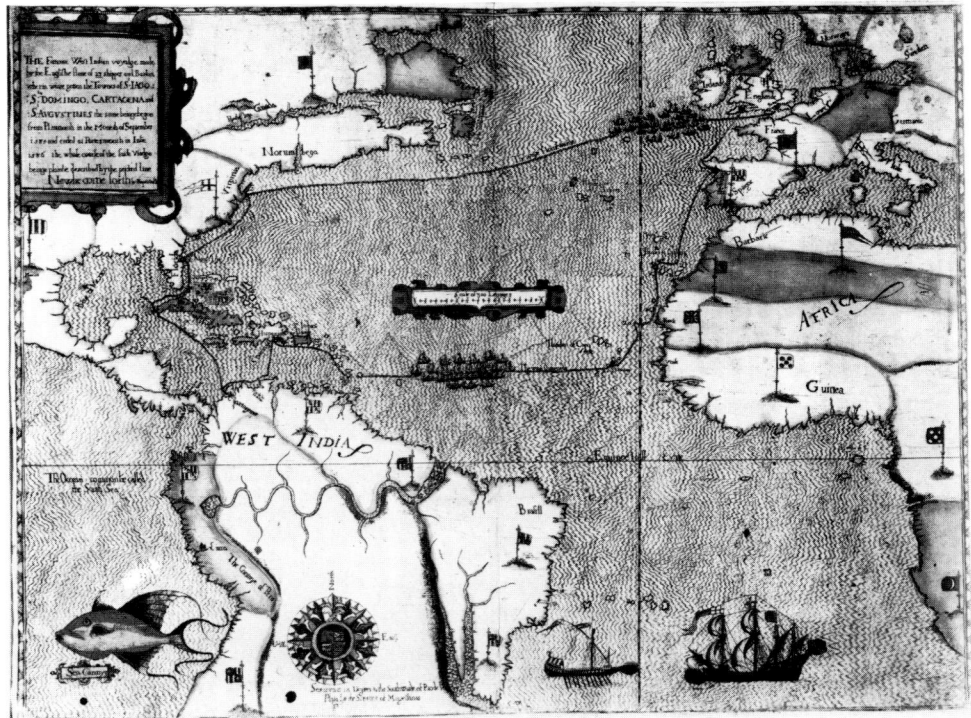

been visited by the Corregidor (governor) of Biscay and his personal guards, all disguised as corn merchants. Once on board he announced the embargo and called on the crew to surrender. They rushed him and his guards, threw them overboard, and set sail. Some of the Spaniards were still clinging to the ship as she got under way and they were taken back on board and brought to England as prisoners. Among them was the Corregidor, still carrying his official instructions explaining that the embargo was a necessary move in the organization of the expedition against England which Philip was already preparing. It was all that was needed. In the fury of public indignation aroused in England, Elizabeth had no option but to proclaim a retaliatory embargo, issue Letters of general reprisal, and appoint Drake as admiral of a squadron to bring back the arrested corn ships. To augment the strength of the squadron she contributed two of her own ships, the *Elizabeth Bonaventure* of 600 tons and the *Aid* of 250 tons.

It was the largest and strongest squadron yet raised in England as a private venture and including the two royal vessels consisted of twenty-one ships and eight pinnaces, with a regular military force of ten companies of soldiers. With Drake sailed Martin Frobisher as his vice-admiral and Francis Knollys as his rear-admiral. The military force was commanded by Lieutenant-General Christopher Carleill.

We have Drake's campaign plan for this Indies voyage, with dates, towns to be attacked, and his estimated value of the booty he would capture and the ransoms he would exact. He had first to go to Spain to liberate the corn ships, a direct order in his commission from the Queen, and was thereafter to plan his own campaign. The expedition sailed from Plymouth on 14 September 1585 and arrived at Vigo in Spain on

27 September. The embargo on the corn ships had already been lifted on 15 September by order of the King, probably because he feared a violent response by the English. Having filled up with stores, Drake left Spain on 8 October and sailed to the Cape Verde Islands off the west coast of Africa. Here, being denied fresh water, he razed the towns of Santiago and Porto Praya. After crossing the Atlantic he planned to arrive at Domenica, sack the town of Margarita ('20 guns, 10,000 ducats'), then sail to Hispaniola and San Domingo ('Many pearls, much spoil, 500,000 ducats'); Santa Marta ('10,000 ducats'); Cartagena ('20 guns, 1,000,000 ducats'); Nombre de Dios ('1,000,000 ducats'); Panama ('1,000,000 ducats'); Isle of Pearls ('a great prey'); the coast of Honduras ('up to 20 Spanish frigates, many rich men and ransom them for 100,000 ducats'); and Havana ('such store of hides and sugar as is to be found ready'). He expected to reach England at the end of the voyage on 10 June 1586.

It proved to be much too ambitious a programme. Drake had made no allowance for the inevitable delays which occur on such expeditions — storms at sea, epidemics among the crews, the long drawn-out arguments with local officials over the size of the ransoms, losses in action, and so on. Although on his return to England the expedition was claimed a triumphant success, in terms of plunder by which the merchants who financed the expedition judged success or failure, the result was a disappointment. In the final audit, after paying the seamen and soldiers their one-third share of the plunder, there remained around £46,000 to set against the cost to the merchants of the expedition up to the day it sailed of £60,000.

Drake had more or less followed his proposed route up to Cartagena, but by then his original timing had slipped by several weeks. After capturing the city and negotiating a ransom which was but a fraction of the amount he expected, he called a council of officers. There had been serious losses in men from disease and battle, and time was running out. With Drake's assent the council decided not to risk the further losses which attacks on Nombre de Dios, Panama, and Havana would inevitably exact, and they agreed to return to England. Already the expedition had passed Drake's expected date of arrival home.

Although the financial return was poor, there were other considerations to be weighed in the final balance. As well as Santiago and Porto Praya in the Cape Verde Islands Drake had destroyed San Domingo and Cartagena, two of the principal Spanish cities in the West Indies and Spanish Main. He had ballasted his ships with more than 240 captured guns, had razed the forts in which they were mounted, had destroyed or captured a great deal of Spanish shipping, and all without the appearance of a single Spanish warship to dispute his attacks. No Spanish ship had sailed from the Americas to Spain carrying the treasure on which Philip depended to finance his widespread operations in Europe. Intelligence from Spain reaching London on 15 May 1586 reported:

> The Bank of Seville is broke:
> The Bank of Venice also very likely . . .
> General speech that the King of Spain will make a great army for England of
> 800 sail of ships but as yet is seen but small preparation, and is only a Spanish
> brag, and very unlikely in many years for him to provide shipping, mariners,
> and soldiers for such an army unless the French assist him.

The effect in Europe when Drake's expedition returned unscathed in July 1586 was

Drake's squadron in Santiago Bay in the Cape Verde Islands at the start of his Indies voyage.

an amazement that so blatant a challenge to Spanish sea power should go unanswered, particularly as the Americas were so vital in financing Philip's ambitions. It was beginning to look as though Spain was vulnerable to English reprisal at sea in the very years that Philip's plans for the huge Armada had become the wonder of western Europe. The effects of Drake's depredations were also felt in the Netherlands. Parma's capture of Antwerp in August 1585 was a success that gave him some promise that the Dutch rebellion was on its last legs. But with the timely help of reinforcements and cash from Elizabeth, Dutch resistance had rallied and managed not only to contain Parma's army but also during the winter to cut off his access to the local provisions he needed to feed his men. A starving army became a new worry to face Parma in his campaign. With Philip unable to provide help from his empty Treasury, Parma had to try to arrange new loans from European financiers.

Again we can see the influence of Drake's expedition, as Parma wrote: 'They are drawing their purse strings very tight and will make no accommodation. The most contemplative of them ponder much over this success of Drake.' In his financial desperation even the King of Spain himself was unable to raise a loan of half a million ducats and it was being said in Paris that he was bankrupt. But the most telling fact of all was that, despite the apparent vastness of Spanish sea power, it had taken Santa Cruz nearly six months following Drake's descent on the Spanish coast to raise a squadron of warships and sail in pursuit, by which time Drake was on his way home. It was not the best of advertisements of Spanish naval efficiency. Even Burghley, never one of Drake's admirers, could write: 'Truly Sir Francis Drake is a fearful man to the King of Spain.'

Opposite: At Santiago Drake had been denied fresh water for his ships and he sacked the town in revenge. English troops are seen advancing on the right.

4 Mary Stuart

The Queen of Scotland, exiled from her native land and held prisoner in England, was executed at Fotheringay Castle on 18 February 1587. Before she laid her head on the block her ladies-in-waiting took off her black dress, as was the custom at such executions. Beneath it she was wearing a red bodice and petticoat, the colour of martyrdom. But Mary Stuart was no true martyr. She was not dying because she was a practising Roman Catholic in a Protestant country but because she had been privy to more than one plot to assassinate her cousin, the Queen of England, and in English minds that was treason. Poor, pathetic Mary. Although she was the dowager Queen of France, the Queen of Scotland, and the legitimate heir to the throne of England, she had thrown away all her chances in life through her intemperate behaviour. Perhaps it was not entirely her fault, for since the age of six she had been brought up in the Court of Henry II of France, the most dissolute in Europe. It was a Court dominated by intrigue, by debauchery, and even by murder, most of it orchestrated by the Queen, Catherine de Medici, who even took a delight in corrupting her own children.

In England, following Mary's execution, there was no sudden Catholic uprising as had been feared; indeed, in London and other cities and towns, bonfires were lit and church bells rung. The Queen and her Privy Council recognized this as no more than surface rejoicing; deeper down there was anxiety as to the reaction in Scotland and, perhaps even more menacing, in France, Rome, and Spain. There was a good deal of fury in Scotland at the beheading of their young King's mother, even though she had disowned him because of his removal from her care at birth and his religious upbringing in the Church of Scotland. There was much Scottish talk of an invasion of the north of England in the hope of raising the English Catholics, but it foundered on the inability of the Scottish nobles to pull together in such an act of aggression. Elizabeth did what she could to take the heat out of their anger by sending William Davison, one of her principal Secretaries of State, to the Tower, accused of forwarding to Fotheringay her warrant for the execution without her express consent. And the Privy Council took the additional precaution of mobilizing the fleet, unusual during the winter months, to keep watch in the English Channel in case Henry, Duke of Guise, Mary Stuart's cousin in France, should be tempted to stir up a Catholic uprising by landing his forces in England.

France had too many troubles of its own to react violently to Mary's execution, even though she had been a Queen of France. Henry of Valois sat too uneasily on his throne to take any risks. The House of Lorraine, at whose head stood the formidable Duke of Guise and his equally formidable brother the Cardinal, raised an outcry and

Henry of Lorraine, Duke of Guise, a drawing of around 1585. Mary Stuart's cousin and a powerful ally, he was also the leader of the Holy League and Philip of Spain's candidate to succeed Henry III as King of France. He was assassinated at Blois at the end of 1588.

clamoured for retaliation. They were the leaders of the Holy League, heavily subsidized by Philip of Spain, with a good claim to the throne of France when Henry, the last of the Valois kings, died. Henry knew well enough the threat to France that Spanish influence on the other side of the English Channel would pose, and he had no wish to see his Guise rivals, with Spain behind them, making any move against England. He was able to dampen down the French enthusiasm for vengeance against England stirred up by the Guise brothers. Mary Stuart had never been popular in France, which had not yet forgotten or forgiven the de Chastelard affair, and she had obviously been an embarrassment to Elizabeth. If he, the King of France, took no active steps of disapproval, perhaps he could hope that with Mary's removal his relations with England might well begin to sail into smoother waters.

If it had been expected that the reaction in Rome to Mary's execution would be particularly virulent, the actions of Pope Sixtus V, who had succeeded to the papacy in 1585, took everyone by surprise. Beyond arranging a solemn Mass to be sung in St. Peter's, Rome, there was little else he could do. As Pope he was of course bound by the earlier Papal Bull imposed by Pius V in 1570 declaring Queen Elizabeth a heretic, and as the religious leader of the Counter-Reformation movement he supported wholeheartedly Philip's 'Enterprise of England'. But on the more secular side he had made no secret of his admiration of the Queen of England as a woman of courage and political skill. His own champion for the restoration of the true faith had to be Philip of Spain, the only possible leader in the field, but he could not help drawing a comparison between the swift and successful English retaliations at sea against Spanish insult and the slow steps of Philip towards the launch of the campaign that was to be the downfall of the Reformation. Nor was he impressed by the immediate Spanish reaction to Mary's execution, which was to request an advance on the Pope's promised gift to Philip when England was invaded. What Sixtus wanted to see was deeds, not more requests for money.

Without some positive backing from Paris and Rome, there was little that Philip could do on his own. Mary Stuart's execution had removed the last chance of a Catholic succession in England without recourse to war, for her son James, now Elizabeth's heir, was of the Scottish Church, even more anti-Catholic than English Protestantism. As Philip saw it, the only option left to him was to press ahead as fast as possible with the assembly of the Armada and its launch against England.

It was a prospect which caused many doubts in his mind. What if the English Catholics did not rise in revolt against Elizabeth to assist his invasion force? His operational plans counted on such an uprising, not because it was needed as an excuse for Spanish aggression but because England was too large a country to be overrun by a Spanish army alone. It was not an encouraging sign that the execution of their titular queen had evoked no firm response from the English Catholics. Philip had been bled white financially by the interminable war against Protestantism in the Netherlands and he had no wish to hang a similar millstone around his neck with a long war in England. And how, so deeply in debt as he already was, was the cost of the Armada to be met? Since Drake's raid on the Spanish Main and the West Indies the flow of treasure from the Americas had been stopped, even if only temporarily; his personal credit was exhausted; there were no financiers in Europe prepared to accommodate him with additional loans. Finally, what certainty was there that a Spanish fleet, even one as large as he contemplated, could meet and defeat an English fleet in English

The execution of Mary Queen of Scots at Fotheringay Castle in February 1587. She had been implicated in the Babington plot to assassinate Queen Elizabeth who, albeit reluctantly, had no other course but to sign the warrant for her execution.

Den VIII february werde onthalst Maria
Stuart Schots Coninginne s'lewende Roomsch Catho-
lyck Hebbende gesocht veel onrusten aen te richten haer schoon
meester te maecken van Engelant t'dwelck haer vanden raet
ofte parlement volcomelyck werde vertoont, Anno 1587.

Metren XIII fol. XIII en XIIII. b

waters? He was under no illusions as to the extent of English sea power in northern waters and was fully aware of the implications of the new English warship design and their long-barrelled guns. He was not known throughout Europe as Philip the Prudent for nothing, but he recognized that the time had now come to put prudence to the test even in the face of his doubts.

He had asked Santa Cruz and Alexander Farnese, Duke of Parma, each to produce plans for the conquest of England, together with estimates of their cost. Santa Cruz's plan recommended that the whole operation, naval and military, be mounted from Spain, without using the Spanish army in the Netherlands, and with himself in overall command. It would require a total war fleet of 150 galleons, forty galleys, and six galleasses, with some 300 auxiliary vessels ranging from the largest merchant ships to pinnaces and sloops. This Armada, he estimated, would require 30,000 sailors and could carry an army of 64,000 soldiers, which, he thought, would be a sufficient force to defeat all resistance that the English could put up afloat and ashore. He made lists of the heavy and light guns needed for the ships, the number of weapons to be carried by the soldiers, and the amount of provisions required for a campaign which would probably last for eight months. His estimate of the cost was fractionally under four million ducats (one gold ducat was approximately equivalent to an English sovereign), a sum that was not only wildly optimistic but infinitely more than Spain could ever raise. And from where, Philip wondered, were the 150 galleons to come? Even with all the galleons he could cajole from the Mediterranean states, added to those he already had, he would have only about one-fifth of the number that Santa Cruz thought necessary.

Parma's plan was simpler, though in Philip's eyes equally unsound. Parma recommended that the whole operation be mounted from the Netherlands without the need of any fleet from Spain, with of course himself in overall command. He proposed to use his existing army of 30,000 men, lifted from the Flanders coast to England in the course of a single night, in a fleet of some 600 barges. All he would need from Spain was a reinforcement of 30,000 soldiers to hold his positions in the Netherlands while his present army conquered England. The two essentials for the success of his plan were, firstly, an uprising by the English Catholics in support of his military operations in England, and, secondly, complete surprise in the crossing of his army from Flanders to the Thames estuary. He did not explain in his submission to Philip how he proposed to gather together 600 barges and 30,000 troops at one place on the coast without the English and the Dutch noticing that something unusual was taking place and drawing the correct conclusion. There would, he thought, be no difficulty in provisioning his army once he was ashore, for England was agriculturally rich and well able to provide all the cattle, corn, and other produce needed to feed his army, especially as he would mount his operation during the summer months.

He would need to capture a sheltered Dutch port for the assembly of the barges, but to a soldier with his reputation such an operation should produce no real difficulty. He thought that Brill and Flushing, the best of the available ports on the Flanders coast, were probably beyond his reach as both were strongly garrisoned by English troops, but Sluys, just along the coast, offered some possibilities. It was not the best of ports, as it had partially silted up during recent years, but it still had a narrow and navigable channel connecting it with the open sea. Parma planned to expand the existing canal system there to bring a much greater advantage.

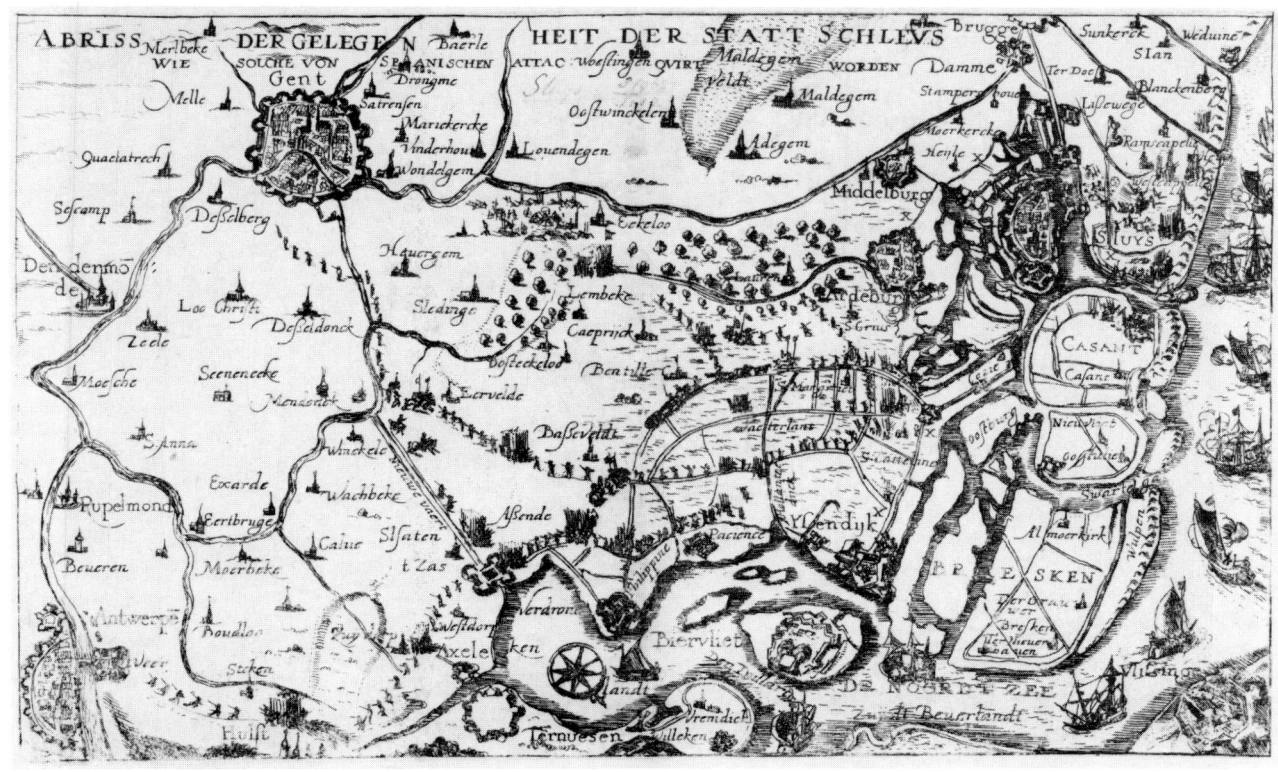

In the event it took Parma two months and considerable numbers of killed and wounded before the garrison of Sluys was forced to surrender. Without delay, he rounded up as much local labour as was available to assist his army in digging a new canal from Sluys to Nieuport, a distance of fifteen miles. When completed and linked to the existing system he would be able to move barges from the Scheldt to Dunkirk, sheltered throughout from the open sea by the coastal dunes. He still had time enough. Sluys fell to him in August 1587 and the earliest date for an invasion of England had already slipped by a year into 1588. With a favourable wind and tide, Parma reckoned that he could lift his army from Dunkirk to England during the dark hours of a single night.

Philip had no difficulty in seizing on the weaknesses of both of these plans. He could rule out that of Santa Cruz on the straightforward ground of physical impossibility; to assemble a fleet of more than 500 ships and to raise an army of 64,000 men would in those days be far beyond the capacity of the whole Continent of Europe together, let alone Spain on her own. And even if Philip could mobilize all the resources of all the gunfounders in Europe, the total output of weapons in the time remaining would still fall short of the number required by Santa Cruz. If he accepted the estimate of the cost of just under four million ducats, which he was by no means prepared to do, it would mean pledging the annual income in treasure from the Americas for

A Dutch sixteenth-century map showing Sluys and its surroundings.

A ball at the Court of Henry III of France at Fontainebleau. The favourite son of Catherine de Medici, he left the government of France largely in the hands of his mother and his favourites while he devoted himself to a life of pleasure.

Opposite: Catherine de Medici of France. She dominated the notorious Court of her husband, Henry II, in which Mary Queen of Scots was brought up. Her malign influence lasted until her death in 1589.

years ahead. And he might have some difficulty finding lenders who would be prepared to risk such a vast sum on such an uncertain adventure.

The flaws in Parma's plan were very obvious. Above all there was the complete impossibility of assembling an army of 30,000 men and a fleet of 600 barges on the Flanders coast in the secrecy which was an essential condition of the plan. There were too many Dutch and English already in the country, to say nothing of the merchants with wagging tongues who thronged the ports of that stretch of the European coast, to make that secrecy remotely possible. Perhaps Philip had some doubt as to whether Parma would not use the 30,000 additional men he demanded to reinforce his existing troops rather than to embark on the gamble of an invasion of England. The war in the Netherlands was still dragging on without much sign yet of a successful conclusion; could Parma perhaps be thinking of his reputation as the general who never lost a battle, let alone a war? It might be an ignoble thought but a prudent leader had to weigh in the balance all the possibilities, however remote they might be.

There was no alternative for Philip but to produce his own plan, which proved to be a combination of the two. It was to force the English Channel with the best and largest fleet that Spain could raise, carrying as many troops as the available space in the ships would allow. Such a fleet could be expected to sink or disable some English ships. Parma was to have his army and its necessary barges assembled on the Flanders coast and ready for embarkation by the time Santa Cruz arrived, at a place to be arranged between the two by the interchange of messengers as the fleet advanced. Parma's army, reinforced by the troops carried in the fleet, would then be convoyed by the whole Armada to the English coast and put ashore at the most suitable landing place, perhaps Margate, perhaps the Thames estuary, or even the Essex coast, depending upon the conditions of wind and tide. Santa Cruz was to remain with his ships in the Channel to protect Parma's lines of communication, and would hope to defeat the remains of the English fleet after the mauling it would have received in the preliminary battles. Santa Cruz was to command the seaborne element of the operation, Parma was to command the military campaign from the moment of his army being put ashore in England.

It was certainly the only possible plan with any chance of success, though even then it begged a number of questions. Its weakness lay in the uncertainty of the timing of the arrival of Santa Cruz at the place of embarkation and of Parma's ability to be there complete with army and barges as the ships arrived. If the English fleet had not been defeated or scattered during the Armada's passage up the Channel, it was certain that no time could be wasted waiting for the junction of the two forces to be made. An undefeated English fleet could cause havoc if the embarkation were unduly delayed. And perhaps there was an element of doubt about the two chosen commanders. Both had enjoyed brilliant careers in their chosen profession. At the same time both were grandees of Spain, an aristocratic *élite* immensely proud and immensely jealous of personal honours and glory. In their individual plans both had put themselves forward as sole overall commander of the whole expedition. It was vital to the success of Philip's plan that the two worked selflessly and harmoniously together during the critical period of the embarkation and passage to England of the army of invasion. And finally there was still the English fleet. There was no doubt in Spanish naval minds that their only hope rested in their ability somehow to fight at close quarters where their heavy short-range guns could inflict the maximum damage. And how was this to be achieved against

Spanish fishermen hauling netted tuna fish ashore outside the walled city of Cadiz. Salted and dried fish was an important part of the victuals of all navies at this period.

the new breed of English warships with their longer-range guns? Spanish captains, and indeed most of the countries of southern Europe which were contributing to the Armada, recognized that to be certain of success they had to trust that God was on the Spanish side and would be prepared to intervene with a miracle should it prove necessary.

The execution of Mary Stuart forced Philip's hand for he could see plainly enough that time was fast running out for him. Since the beginnings of his 'Enterprise of England' he had adopted a step-by-step approach, consolidating each step before advancing the next. Now, in the spring of 1587, a new burst of royal energy revitalized the expedition. An endless stream of commands and exhortations issued from his Palace of the Escurial: to his chosen commanders to speed their preparations by every means in their power; to the great arsenals of Spain to cast more guns for the ships and provide more powder and more small arms for the soldiers; to the carpenters and coopers of the Algarve to speed up the making of oak casks for the vast quantities of fresh water, provisions, and powder that so large an expedition would require; to the victuallers to increase the stocks of biscuit, salt beef, and salt pork; to the tuna fisheries of the south to redouble their effort in the catching and salting down of fish for the meatless days demanded by the Roman faith; to his Mediterranean allies to hurry along with the sailing to Spain of every ship, particularly galleons, that they could spare. Throughout Spain, along the Biscay coast, and in the Mediterranean, the King of Spain's urgency was reflected in a furious energy, all bent towards a single end. The rest of Europe watched and waited.

5 Cadiz 1587

It was quite impossible, even with the use of cover plans, to keep a secret in Europe in the sixteenth century. All nations had their agents scattered throughout Europe and they had no difficulties in smuggling their reports back to their masters. In addition there was a host of freelance ships' captains, merchants and travellers always eager to pass on what they had observed or been told during their journeys. It was not possible to hide the increased naval and military activity in Spanish ports, the concentration of warships at Lisbon, the chartering of merchant ships as auxiliaries, the movements of troops, the assembling of stores of all descriptions, and not to connect it all with the imminent despatch of an important expedition. In England, Burghley's postbag was swollen with intelligence reports from Spain, all telling the same story. Reports from the Netherlands were equally explicit. Here also the collection of stores and barges, the first essential for an attempt at invasion, could not fail to be noticed. Stories spread in Spain that the fleet being so assiduously prepared was destined for the Far East. And from Parma himself came stories that he was contemplating an assault on Walcheren in the Netherlands. Neither were believed, and in England and elsewhere in Europe there was never any doubt that it could mean anything but the final preparations for Philip's invasion of England.

Yet still there had been no specific declaration of war, and there were many in both England and Spain who believed that both Elizabeth and Philip had no real stomach for a fight, not from any fear of battle but because both considered that the best interests of their countries were better served by peace even if it remained an uneasy one. It was certainly true of Elizabeth, mainly on economic grounds, and possibly so of Philip for the same reason, though he had greatly narrowed his options by putting himself forward as the champion of the Counter-Reformation.

As the winter of 1586–7 proceeded and the reports from the English spies grew more specific and urgent, all hope of an arrangement between the two sovereigns faded. The Queen, sitting with her Privy Council, was forced to act, if only in self-defence, and gave her blessing to two expeditions against the Spanish preparations. The first was the despatch of a small squadron, commanded by an unwilling Hawkins, into the Atlantic, presumably to look for the possible return of a Spanish *flota* bringing to Spain the treasure of the New World. Curiously there is no mention of this in the English State Papers, probably because it was completely unproductive, but reports in the equivalent Spanish Papers leave no doubt that Hawkins's mission did in fact take place. The second expedition was much more ambitious, the despatch of a larger and more powerful squadron, to which the Queen contributed four of her best ships and two pinnaces,

The city and dockyard of Seville, painted by Sanchez Coello towards the end of the sixteenth century. The port of Seville controlled the sailing and protection of the annual flota *bringing home to Spain the treasure gained in America and the West Indies.*

to operate on the coast of Spain itself. The orders for the expedition were agreed in March 1587. Drake was to command it, and according to Walsingham his instructions were:

> to impeach the joining together of the King of Spain's fleet out of their several ports, to keep victuals from them, to follow them in case they should be come forward towards England or Ireland, and to cut off as many of them as he could, and impeach their landing, as also to set upon such as should either come out of the West or East Indies into Spain, or go out of Spain thither.

The conduct of those instructions was left entirely to his own discretion, and he was also given leave 'to distress the [Spanish] ships within the havens themselves.'

To a leader of Drake's experience and temperament these were the perfect instructions. He lost no time in collecting his squadron which, when it sailed, consisted of sixteen well-armed ships and seven pinnaces. The expedition was, as usual, organized as a commercial venture, with merchants of London and Plymouth providing most of the ships, though it was certainly under the close control of the Government through the authority delegated by the Queen to Drake. As in his previous expedition to the Indies in 1585–6, he embarked a military force of ten companies (1,000 soldiers) for any land operations.

Never was a man more eager to get quickly to sea than Drake. Whether he had some private foreknowledge, possibly through his friend Walsingham who was privy to the Queen's decisions in Council, or whether he was acting on his own knowledge of Elizabeth's leanings towards peace rather than war, he worked unceasingly at getting his squadron fully manned and provisioned in the shortest possible time. He sailed from Plymouth on 2 April 1587 with his original instructions intact and he was only just in time. Hardly were his ships over the horizon when a messenger arrived from London with new orders. Recent intelligence out of Spain seemed to indicate that Philip was slowing down his preparations and Elizabeth took this to show a desire on his part for a peaceful understanding. The new orders instructed Drake to 'forbear to enter forcibly any of the said King's ports or havens; or to offer any violence to any of his towns or shipping within harbouring, or to do any act of hostility upon the land'. It was a restriction that would have torn the whole heart out of the projected operation had it reached Drake in time.

As it was an official order from the Queen it was sent on in a pinnace in the hope of reaching Drake's squadron during its passage to Spain. It is a curious little story. The pinnace was supplied by Sir William Wynter, one of the senior admirals of England, and the messenger was said to have been a base-born son of John Hawkins employed at the Court through his father's influence. The pinnace was said to have been delayed by storms, was therefore unable to reach Drake, and returned a few days later with a ship which it had captured, valued at £5,000. The prize money was shared equally between Wynter and Hawkins. As there had been a personal vendetta between the two men for many years, the affair gave rise to malicious gossip that Wynter's half share of £2,500 was in reality a bribe from Hawkins, a friend of Drake, to make sure that the pinnace should not find him and that Drake should continue on his way with only his original orders to guide his activities. Be that as it may, there was nothing now that Queen or Council could do to stop him.

The first rendezvous for the squadron was Cape Roca, known to seamen as the

The royal commission to Sir Francis Drake appointing him to command the fleet for the attack on Cadiz in 1587 and empowering him to 'punish and correct with all severity' all who offended against his discipline.

Rock of Lisbon, at the mouth of the River Tagus. By mid-April the whole squadron had arrived, reinforced by two armed ships met at sea and conscripted into the squadron. A Flemish merchant ship they encountered on her passage home volunteered the information that she had recently left Cadiz, where her crew had seen an unusual number of ships and a vast accumulation of stores and provisions. As an opening target it was too good an opportunity to be missed. Three days later the squadron, apart from a few of the slower ships which arrived later, reached Cadiz and Drake, against the advice of William Borough, his vice-admiral and an old navy officer of high reputation, attacked without waiting for the stragglers. It was an incident which caused arguments and bad blood between the two men, the first of several disagreements which culminated in a later accusation of mutiny. As Cadiz was well defended and with a large inner harbour approached from the outer only by a narrow channel, Borough's caution is perhaps understandable. But he did not know Drake and his methods, and mistook his dash and skill in sudden attack for an inexperience and impetuosity that could well lead the entire expedition to disaster.

It took two days for the squadron to inflict considerable loss and damage to the shipping in Cadiz and an even greater loss in the stores so far collected for onward passage to the Armada gathering in Lisbon. In his despatch to Walsingham, written on 7 May, Drake wrote:

> The 16th [26 April N.S.] we met all together at the Rock [of Lisbon] and the 19th [29 April] we arrived into the Road of Cadiz, in Spain, where we found sundry great ships, some laden, some half-laden, and some ready to be laden with the King's provisions for England. We stayed there until the 21st [1 May], in which meantime we sank a Biscayan of 1,200 tons, burnt a ship of the Marquess of Santa Cruz of 1,500 tons, and 31 ships more of 1,000, 800, 600, 400 to 200 tons the piece, carried away four with us laden with provisions, and departed thence at our pleasure, with as much honour as we could wish.

The official Spanish report of their losses from the attack admits to twenty-four ships, including Santa Cruz's galleon, of which eighteen were burnt and six captured. The value of the losses was assessed at 172,000 ducats. No doubt the authorities at Cadiz kept their estimate on the low side for the same reason that Drake in his despatch put his on the high side. Both had to account to their masters for their actions.

Drake, if pleased at the extent of the damage he had done, was no less amazed at the evidence of Philip's preparations for an invasion which he had seen all around him. In the same despatch he wrote:

> I assure your honour the like preparation was never heard of nor known as the King of Spain hath and daily maketh to invade England. He is allied with mighty Princes and Dukes in the Straits [Mediterranean] of whom (besides the forces in his own dominions) he is to have great aid shortly, and his provisions of bread and wines are so great as will suffice 40,000 men a whole year, which, if they be not impeached before they join, will be very perilous.

To hammer the message home he added a scribbled postcript: 'I dare not a'most write unto your honour of the great forces we hear the King of Spain hath in the Straits. Prepare in England strongly, and most by sea. Stop him now, and stop him ever. Look well to the coast of Sussex.'

The defence of Cadiz against English attack, painted by Francisco Zurbarán for Philip IV's Buen Retiro palace (now in the Prado). In the foreground are the governor and chief officers of the port, while English ships can be seen attacking in the background.

There had been in Cadiz during Drake's attack a squadron of seven galleys commanded by Don Pedro de Açuna, and four others under separate command. Conditions during the two days were ideal for galley warfare—sheltered waters and a fitful wind that on occasions died away to force sailing ships to anchor to stop drifting. Yet for all their manoeuvrability, their speed under oars, their independence of the wind, they were no match for the broadsides of a sailing warship even when anchored. The galley's guns were mounted in the bows, where there was room for only three or four, whereas the sailing ship's 20 to 25 guns were mounted on the broadside. In continued attacks the galleys failed to hit a single English ship, and each time they were driven back and suffered considerable damage. Santa Cruz had asked for forty galleys to accompany the Armada; perhaps it was this experience of their vulnerability when faced with broadside warships that, in the event, caused the forty to be reduced to four.

Leaving Cadiz in early May, Drake intercepted an order from the Indies Office in Seville to Don Juan Martínez de Recalde, instructing him to return to Lisbon because of Drake's presence on the coast. Recalde was commanding a squadron cruising off Cape St. Vincent to cover the *flota* bringing the annual treasure from America. He was a veteran of many naval wars and one of the most distinguished sea officers of Spain, already selected by Philip to be Santa Cruz's vice-admiral for the Armada. This order, revealing to Drake Recalde's present cruising ground, opened up another great target. The English squadron was powerful enough to overwhelm Recalde if they should meet; to sink or capture his ships and perhaps bring him back a prisoner would not only be an outstanding blow for England but might also lead to the capture of a few rich prizes from the *flota*. Calms and contrary winds delayed Drake's passage, and by the time he rounded Cape St. Vincent Recalde had received a duplicate of the order and had withdrawn to Lisbon and safety from the threat of Drake's superior force.

It was a disappointment, but there was still the clause in Drake's instructions, 'to impeach the joining together of the King of Spain's fleet out of their several ports, to keep victuals from them', and for this he needed a safe haven on the stretch of coast between St. Vincent and Cadiz from which he could operate. He had a look at the port of Lagos but found it too strongly defended to be attempted, and decided instead that the anchorage at Sagres, just east of Cape St. Vincent, would best suit his purpose. It was used by ships sailing west from the Mediterranean and east into the Mediterranean, both anchoring there to wait for a favourable wind for the onward voyage. It had plenty of fresh water for refilling casks, good facilities for careening ships to clean the weed from their bottoms, and accommodation ashore where sick seamen would have a better chance of recovery. It was strongly defended by the guns of Sagres Castle, built on the top of the 200-foot cliffs surrounding the anchorage.

The castle, though formidable, was by no means impregnable and Drake in person led his land force in the attack. It surrendered after the main gate had been breached by fire, with a loss of only two men killed in the attacking force. Three smaller forts in the vicinity were easily captured and razed to the ground, and Drake was master of the anchorage.

With the English squadron in possession of Sagres, no ship could sail west out of the Mediterranean without inevitable capture, and none attempted it. At Cartagena, inside the Mediterranean and anxiously awaited by Santa Cruz at Lisbon, were six large Levanters (merchant ships) under the command of Don Diego Pimentel, with four galleasses and two more Levanters expected there from Naples. All twelve carried

A map of Cadiz drawn by William Borough during Drake's attack in 1587. William Borough was Drake's second-in-command and commanded the Golden Lion. *An officer of the old school, he was appalled by Drake's recklessness and the two quarrelled bitterly.*

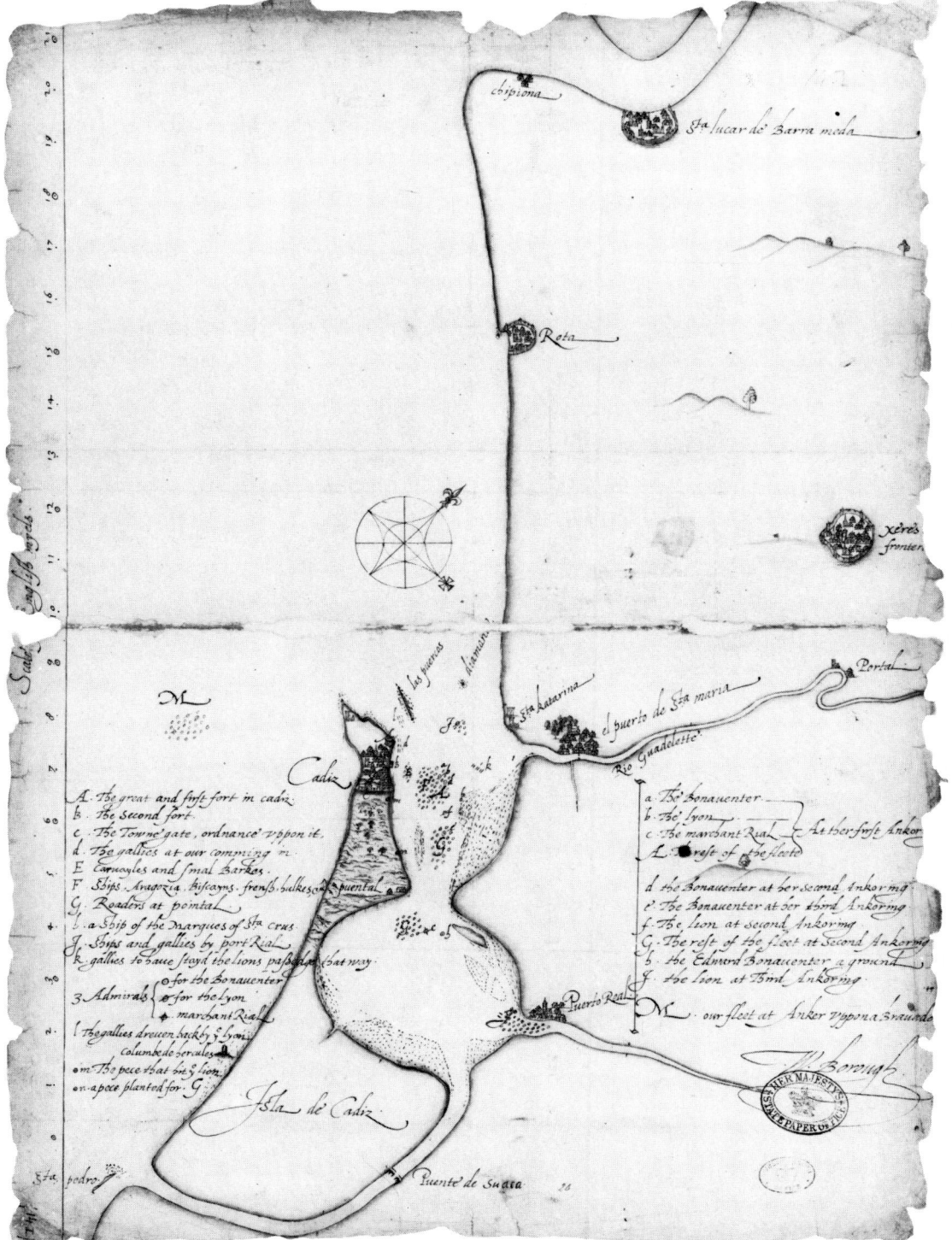

Portrait of Elizabeth Sydenham, attributed to George Gower. She was the daughter and heiress of Sir George Sydenham, and Sir Francis Drake married her as his second wife in 1585.

Opposite: Sir Francis Drake, Vice-Admiral of the English fleet during the battles in the Channel. His formulation of the essential strategy needed to defeat the Spaniards was largely responsible for the victory.

additional guns for the Armada and troops from Italy to swell the invasion force. While they remained inactive in the Mediterranean, Drake swept the seas around the south coast of Spain bare of shipping. Some fifty local ships carrying supplies to Lisbon were captured or sunk, and around the same number of fishing vessels were destroyed with their nets.

A second despatch from Drake to Walsingham made clear the gravity to Spain of these actions:

> . . . there hath happened between the Spaniards, Portingals, and ourselves divers combats, in the which it hath pleased God that we have taken forts, ships, barks, carvels [caravels] and divers other vessels more than a hundred, most laden, some with oars for galleys, planks and timber for ships and pinnaces, hoops and pipe-staves for cask, with many other provisions for this great army. I assure your honour the hoops and pipe-staves were above 16 or 17 hundred tons in weight, which cannot be less than 25 or 30 thousand ton [of provisions] if it had been made in cask ready for liquor, all which I commanded to be consumed into smoke and ashes by fire, which will be unto the King no small waste of his provisions, besides the want of his barks. The nets which we have consumed will cause the people to curse their governors to their faces.

Drake was above all a seaman and knew very well how much in those days ships depended on the casks in which they carried all their drinking water and wine, their salt beef and pork, their flour and powder. The staves he had burned had been of weathered oak ready for making up into casks, and he knew also that there was not enough time to weather newly sawn oak if the Armada were to sail on schedule. He was also well aware that Spain had been driven from the Newfoundland cod fishery and her fishing fleet destroyed some years previously and that she now depended entirely on the Algarve tuna fishery for the fleet's supply of salted fish, an essential part of the victuals in all navies. There was only one thing he regretted from this expedition, that he had failed to capture a rich prize or two to produce a worthwhile dividend for the Queen and the merchants, including himself, who had volunteered their ships.

In the same despatch to Walsingham he looked forward to the ultimate victory and the strategy to achieve it:

> There must be a beginning of any great matter, but the continuing unto the end until it be thoroughly finished yields the true glory . . . God make us all thankful again and again that we have, although it be little, made a beginning on the coast of Spain. If we can thoroughly believe that this which we do is in the defence of our religion and country, no doubt but our merciful God, for his Christ our Saviour's sake, is able and will give us victory, although our sins be red.

There can be no doubt of what Drake was thinking, for the obvious plan was staring him in the face: a break of three or four weeks at home to clean and tallow the ships, to recruit new crews, to replenish with powder, ball, and provisions, and then a return to the Spanish coast for 'the continuing unto the end'. It made good strategic sense.

The work of Drake's expedition was nearly done. While he remained at Sagres he blocked all movement of the reinforcements from the Mediterranean so urgently needed at Lisbon. Possibly as a diversion, possibly as a reconnaissance, Drake took his squadron to Lisbon itself, anchoring there on 20 May within sight of Santa Cruz's headquarters in St. Julian's Castle. He challenged Santa Cruz to come out and fight, but the old admiral, his ships mostly unmanned and still wanting their guns, was powerless. After two days Drake returned to Sagres to allow his sick men to recuperate and to clean and disinfect his ships.

Suddenly, towards the end of May, he disappeared into the blue, sending his sick men home in some of the ships he had taken as prizes. He had heard that a large carrack homeward bound from the East Indies was expected to arrive that month. It might well be the rich prize he so much desired. His destination was the Azores, that Atlantic port at which the trading ships from east and west all called to replenish their provisions before the final stretch home to Spain. He sighted the islands on the morning of 8 June and by the evening was close enough to see a large ship lying in the lee of the land. At daybreak on the 9th she was seen to be under way towards the squadron, presumably under the impression that it must be Spanish, and it was only when she was within gun range that Drake hoisted his colours. She surrendered after a short action and proved to be the carrack for which he was looking.

She was the *San Felipe*, the King of Spain's own ship, and the full value of her cargo when it was sold in England was £113,949 13s. 11d., the equivalent today of several millions of pounds. Even more valuable in the long run were her accounts and

Portrait by Marcus Gheeraerts of William Cecil, Lord Burghley, Queen Elizabeth's Lord High Treasurer and principal minister. He was the leading politician throughout the campaign of the Spanish Armada, building up an extensive system of agents throughout Europe by whom he was kept informed of every Spanish move.

Sir William Cecill knight. Baron
of Burghley Lord high Treasorer of
England, knight of the most noble
order of the Garter and Master of
her Ma[ty] court of wardes and Lyveries.

CORVNV VIA VNA

A German view of Sir Francis Drake. He is shown in armour holding a musket, while a warship is being loaded with powder and ammunition. All the countries of western Europe, Protestant and Catholic, recognized the significance of the campaign of the Spanish Armada.

papers, which revealed the closely guarded secrets of the Portuguese trade in India and the East and opened the eyes of English merchants to the great riches to be earned in that part of the world. It is true that, before the capture of the *San Felipe*, the English Muscovy Company had made some efforts to open a trade in the Far East, but it was the revelations of the *San Felipe's* papers which led to the formation a dozen years later of the English East India Company which, during the two and a half centuries of its existence, had so profound an effect on the development of world trade and the growth of empire.

The capture of the *San Felipe* was the last offensive act of the Cadiz operation. Even if the damage done to the warships designated to form the Armada fleet was less than Drake had hoped, the disruption he had caused to its concentration at Lisbon and the destruction of necessary stores for its maintenance at sea had obviously delayed its sailing for a long time. Philip had intended that his Armada should sail in the summer of 1587. In fact it was delayed for a year, though Philip did not finally accept the fact until December. Santa Cruz had recognized it almost from Drake's initial appearance on the Spanish coast, and he had told the King so.

Unaware of the capture of the *San Felipe*, Santa Cruz had by June at last managed to get the Portuguese galleons fit for sea. His fears mounted for the safety of the *flota* due from the Spanish Main with the annual produce from Peru. He knew that it would first make for the Azores and he suspected that those islands were also the destination of Drake's ships. He sailed from Lisbon at the end of June just as Drake was entering Plymouth Sound with the *San Felipe*. At the Azores Santa Cruz missed the *flota*, which

had been delayed by contrary winds in the Atlantic, and with no news of Drake, spent the next three months at sea in a fruitless search for him.

These English operations, facetiously described as 'the singeing of the King of Spain's beard', were a full justification of the new English philosophy of naval strategy, to take the fight to the enemy and strike at his point of concentration in order to weaken him and deprive him of his command of the sea. Drake in particular understood this. As he wrote to the Privy Council:

> My very good Lords, next under God's mighty protection, the advantage and gain of time and place will be the only and chief means for our good; wherein I most humbly beseech your good Lordships to persevere as you have begun; for that with fifty sail of shipping we shall do more good upon their own coast than a great many more will do here at home.

A valuable lesson learned during the Cadiz expedition was that the broadside warship had nothing to fear from galleys. Thomas Fenner, Drake's former flag captain and now commanding the Queen's *Dreadnought* in this expedition, summed it up in a letter of 27 May written to Walsingham:

> I assure your Honour there is no account to be made of his [Philip's] galleys. Twelve of her Majesty's ships will not make account of all his galleys in Spain, Portugal, and all his dominions within the Straits, although there are 150 in number. If it be to their advantage in a calm, we have made such trial of their accounts that we perfectly see into the depth thereof.

6 Countdown

The winter of 1587–8 was a mixed one for Philip of Spain. One encouraging event was the safe arrival towards the end of the year of the *flota* from the West Indies, much of it so delayed that it had been given up as lost. The treasure it bore was enough to put him in credit again. Another was the reinforcement of the army in the Low Countries with trained troops from Italy, which enabled Parma to report to Philip that he and his army were now at a peak and only awaited the arrival of the Armada to embark and start the invasion. But there was bad news from France where Henry of Guise, Philip's candidate for the succession to the French throne, had been unexpectedly and heavily defeated by the Huguenot Henry of Navarre at Coutras on 20 October. It was a blow to Philip's hopes of a France under the political control of Spain and also represented a considerable cash loss in the arms and other support he had invested in his French hopeful. True, it was only one battle and the Guise star could rise again, though it would once more cost the Spanish Treasury dear.

The greatest of his worries, however, lay in Lisbon where the Armada was gathering. Santa Cruz had not returned from his voyage to the Azores until the end of September, his squadron storm-battered and in need of repair. One galleon had been lost, another was in such poor condition that she was not worth the cost of rebuilding. He was met at Lisbon with an order from the King to put to sea with the Armada and start the operations against England. It was in vain that he argued that the ships were not ready, that he was still awaiting the arrival of guns and essential stores, that the squadron of Biscayans on which he counted had not yet reached Lisbon, that he was still short of trained mariners for the crews, that it would be madness to risk the fleet in a difficult and protracted operation so late in the year.

None of these arguments moved Philip and he continued to insist on immediate action. He had sent for one of his favourites from the fleet to join him in the Escurial, Alonso de Leyva, whom he had appointed as Lieutenant-General of the Armada. He relied on this young and inexperienced hothead to provide him with reasons to ignore the solid good sense of his Commander-in-Chief. Santa Cruz was old and tired, and the long arguments with Philip and de Leyva sapped even more of his failing energy. His almost daily correspondence with the Escurial continued into December before Philip at last had to agree that Santa Cruz was right and that the sailing of the Armada must be delayed into 1588. The elderly Marquis was given until March to complete his preparations down to the last man, the last gun, the last stowage of all stores.

Worn out by the worries of the Armada, Santa Cruz died on 9 February. He had been failing in health for some weeks and had been losing his grip under the constant

The Escurial, the great palace and monastery built by Philip of Spain in the foothills of the Guadarramas. Here he produced his plans for the 'Enterprise of England'.

prodding from Philip. Essential repairs to the ships were undertaken too late and too slowly; there was confusion in the allocations of guns, some ships receiving twice their quota, others none at all; discipline was lax and crews deserted in their hundreds. Through de Leyva, now back in the fleet, Philip was kept informed of what was happening in Lisbon, and even before the old admiral died the King was in communication with the man he had selected to be the new Commander-in-Chief, the Duke of Medina Sidonia.

It was an odd choice. Alonso Perez de Guzman el Bueno was the seventh Duke of Medina Sidonia, the oldest duchy in Spain, and as such was one of the grandest of Spanish grandees. An earlier duke had earned the distinction of *el Bueno*, the good, and subsequent dukes had automatically tacked it on to their title without necessarily qualifying for it by their actions or behaviour. The present holder succeeded to the title when he was five years old and on the death of his grandfather inherited one of the greatest fortunes in Europe. At the age of fifteen he was betrothed to a four-year-old Mendoza princess, daughter of the Prince of Eboli, and seven years later the Pope granted him a dispensation for the consummation of the marriage. At one time it was widely believed in Spain that Philip had become her lover because of the continual favours he showered on the duke.

Medina Sidonia's earlier correspondence with Philip does not show him in a good light, mainly pleading his poverty and appealing for financial favours. He was always eager to accept new appointments with grand titles but avoided any financial obligations attached to them. On the basis of his letters to the King it is impossible to think of him but as a man of mean spirit.

Philip drafted Medina Sidonia's letter of appointment three days before Santa Cruz died, creating him Captain General of the Ocean Sea. The title at least must have pleased the duke as he retained it to the day of his death, even though after the Armada returned all the Spanish people openly expressed their contempt for him. But title or no, he tried hard to avoid the responsibility of so important a charge. In a letter to Juan de Idiaquez, the King's secretary, he wrote:

> My health is not equal to such a voyage, for I know by experience of the little
> I have been at sea that I am always seasick and always catch cold. My family
> is burdened with a debt of nine hundred thousand ducats, and I could not spend
> a real [a Spanish penny] in the King's service. Since I have had no experience
> of the sea, or of war, I cannot feel that I ought to command so important an
> enterprise. I know nothing of what the Marquis of Santa Cruz has been doing,
> or of what intelligence he has of England, so I feel I should give but a bad account
> of myself, commanding thus blindly, and being obliged to rely on the advice
> of others, without knowing good from bad, or which of my advisers might want
> to deceive or displace me.

His plea fell on deaf ears. Perhaps Philip recognized in this letter the pattern of so many others he had received from the duke in the past, the same plea of poverty, the same avoidance of responsibility. 'All of what you say,' he wrote in reply, 'I attribute to your excess of modesty. But it is I who must judge of your capabilities and parts, and I am fully satisfied with them.' And in any case, he pointed out, it was too late to change now as his appointment of the duke had already been made public. There

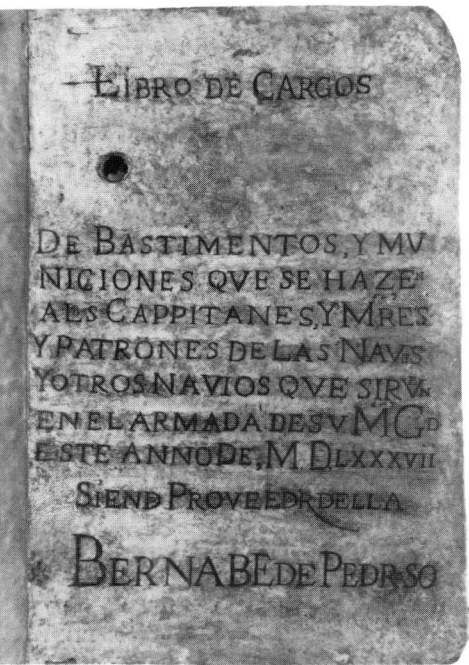
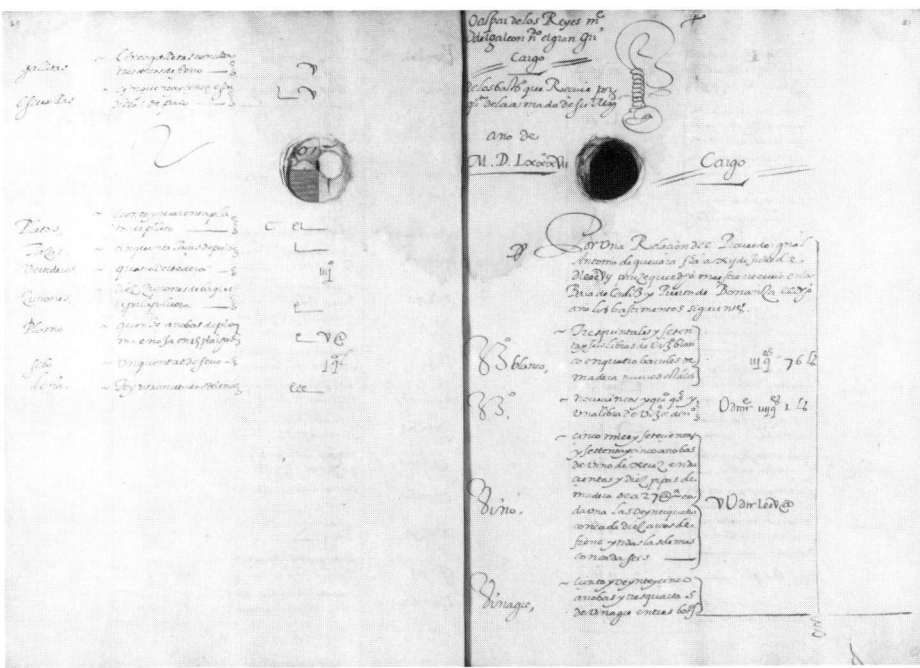

was no option for Medina Sidonia but to leave his orange groves at San Lucar and to travel post-haste to Lisbon.

What he found there appalled him. Although he had little experience of the sea, he could see plainly enough that for the Armada to sail in its present state must spell disaster. His first action was to form a small Council of experienced officers to advise him. It consisted of Juan Martínez de Recalde, Miguel de Oquendo, and Pedro de Valdes, all three able and experienced leaders already selected to command squadrons in the Armada. They worked well with Medina Sidonia in trying to bring some order out of the chaos left by Santa Cruz. Later, after Philip had finally agreed to release the galleons of the Indian Guard for the Armada and they had arrived in Lisbon, Medina Sidonia added the commander of that squadron to the Council. He was Diego Flores de Valdes, a cousin of Pedro and a proud and intensely ambitious man who soon exercised more power over Medina Sidonia than did the original three. His advice was often suspect, and a Council at odds, particularly with a Commander-in-Chief who listened more to one member than to the three others, was not the happiest augury for the success of the expedition.

As winter passed into spring the date for the sailing of the Armada slipped from March to April and from April to May. The chief cause was the shortage of guns, particularly of brass demi-cannons and culverins with their longer range and ship-killing potential. There had been promised deliveries of guns of this type, as compared with the short-range man-killers, from many of the European gunfounders but few, if any, lived up to their delivery dates. The deficiency in weapons was made up by the purchase of existing guns, particularly from merchant ships, and these were mainly iron guns

The front cover and two pages from an Armada cargo book. Every merchant ship in the fleet carried one, giving a list of the provisions loaded on board. This example came from the Gran Grifon, almirante (second-in-command) of the squadron of urcas, which was wrecked on Fair Isle during the voyage home to Spain.

of comparatively short range. When the Armada finally sailed from Lisbon in May few ships had their hoped-for complement of brass guns, and many of the iron guns mounted in their place were not of the quality needed to fight a fleet so well trained and equipped as the English.

Almost as worrying was the condition of the ships and their crews. The ships had been kept in full commission throughout the winter on Philip's orders, ready to sail on the earliest possible date. A major survey ordered by Medina Sidonia and his Council revealed a distressing number of rotted timbers and worm-riddled bottom planking, particularly in the galleons of Portugal. With the crews living permanently on board it was difficult to organize a routine of docking and repair. As much as possible was gradually put in hand and by the time the Armada sailed most of the damaged timbers and bottom planking had been renewed and the sprung masts and yards replaced with new ones.

The crews were in no better shape than the ships. They were subject to the diseases inherent in those days in shipboard life, and although there is no record of an actual epidemic sweeping through the crews the death toll was abnormally high. All the time they were consuming provisions which were supplied for the expedition itself. Replacement was difficult, for Drake's destruction of hoops and pipe-staves during the Cadiz raid had resulted in a shortage of casks suitable for long storage. It was found that after a few weeks in cask the contents turned bad and unfit for consumption because of the leakage of the salt liquor in which they were preserved, the result of using unmatured oak in the casks' construction. Also there was not enough money available to pay the crews and it was hardly surprising that soldiers and seamen deserted at an alarming rate. The desertion of soldiers was of less concern to the Council than that of the sailors. Soldiers were relatively unskilled and numbers could be made up by enlistment and a measure of compulsory service, but the desertion of seamen left a gap that it was more difficult to fill. Their particular skills were only acquired after a long apprenticeship at sea and the ships depended for their safety on those skills.

One of the odder decisions of the Council was to rebuild the towering fore- and aftercastles on some of the more modern galleons and merchant ships. A few had been initially 'race-built' somewhat on the new English pattern, with a longer length-to-beam ratio, a flush deck, and a low forecastle. Most Spanish captains distrusted this new design, preferring the original design of high castles forward and aft to form the equivalent of a welldeck amidships. In their reckoning the two high castles provided protection for the crew from enemy gunfire and also enabled them to fire downwards from the castles on would-be boarders entering over the welldeck. This was the typical fortress mentality of the Spanish soldier and it was the man initially trained as a soldier who still commanded at sea. As the English had discovered, the race-built ship was faster and more weatherly than the older design of high-charged ship but to the Spanish captains these advantages must have counted less than the defensive strength of the traditional castles forward and aft. The Council's decision meant the sacrifice of a knot in speed and a point in sailing closer to the wind, and in the battles fought in the English Channel later in the year the lack of these two qualities cost Philip's Armada dear.

In spite of his continuing difficulties in Lisbon, but mindful of Philip's ceaseless prodding, Medina Sidonia reported to the King in April that the Armada would be ready to sail in another week or two. On the 25th of the month, in the presence of

The Duke of Medina Sidonia. Philip II chose him to succeed Santa Cruz in the command of the Armada fleet, a choice widely criticized in Spain where he was unpopular. He knew nothing of naval strategy and tactics.

Opposite: A Spanish galley, rowing twenty-three oars a side. A squadron of four of these galleys was included in the Spanish fleet which sailed for England in 1588 but all four were forced to abandon the voyage during rough weather in the Bay of Biscay.

Medina Sidonia, his squadron commanders, most of the principal captains and officers, and a vast congregation of the leading citizens, the special standard of the Armada was blessed at a service in the cathedral and carried in procession through the streets of Lisbon. Every soldier and sailor had been to confession and communion and had received a papal absolution of his sins. On 9 May the ships left Lisbon down river towards the sea. The fleet's nominal list showed a strength of 132 ships of a total of 59,190 tons, manned by 8,066 mariners, with 21,621 soldiers embarked. Some hundreds of cavalry horses and draught mules were also carried. This was the strength of the Armada on paper; it was not so great when it reached the English Channel. Officially the Armada was given the name of *la Felicissima*, the most fortunate; but in the Armada itself and to much of Spain it was known as *la Invencible*, the invincible, as an acknowledgement of its size and nature. It was the largest and, on paper, the strongest fleet that the world had ever seen.

One more piece of the jigsaw was still to fall into place. Parma had earlier written to Philip and to Mendoza, the Spanish ambassador in Paris, that before sailing to England with his army he would need a guarantee that France would not attack in the Low Countries while he was engaged in the invasion of England. It was the sort of situation in which Mendoza, a master of intrigue, excelled. Although the King of France was well established in Paris, the city itself was a hotbed of the Holy League. Mendoza's plan was to foment an armed uprising of the League, force the King out of Paris, and place control of the city with the Duke of Guise, the pro-Spanish leader of the Holy League and now materially recovered from his earlier defeat by Henry of Navarre. It all went according to Mendoza's plan. The duke was smuggled into Paris on 9 May. On the 10th he faced the King but was saved from further banishment through the pleading of Catherine de Medici, the King's mother, at the urging of Mendoza. On the 11th the League rose in revolt and drove the King's forces from the streets. By evening the city was in the hands of the mob; the King escaped through an unguarded gate to Chartres; and the Duke of Guise was master of Paris. With the city held by the Holy League, Parma need have no fears of a French invasion.

To give added weight to the League's victory Mendoza announced to the enthusiastic Parisians that the Armada had already left Lisbon and was on its way to England. In fact it was still anchored at the mouth of the Tagus estuary, prevented from putting to sea by a series of onshore gales. It was not until 28 May that the *San Martin*, Medina Sidonia's flagship, was able to lead the fleet out of the estuary and not until the 30th that the last of the Armada ships crossed the estuary bar and reached the open sea. Their rendezvous was the Scilly Islands.

In England, Queen Elizabeth had been under conflicting pressures. Drake, who was back in Plymouth in the summer of 1587 with his prize taken in the Azores, was unhappy that there was no order from the Queen to refit and re-equip his squadron for a second venture against the Spanish mainland. He had seen the extent of the Spanish preparations, had reported them again on his return, and had convinced everyone, including Elizabeth, that this time the Armada was more than rumour and conjecture, it was now a reality. Yet not only had the Queen expressly forbidden him to sail on a second expedition of destruction and disruption but she also refused to mobilize the fleet in spite of all the evidence. Elizabeth has been widely criticized for her decision to pay off the fleet during these anxious months, criticism not so much in England at the time as from the pens of more recent historians, who accuse her of endangering the country through her parsimony and a lack of comprehension of the enormity of the threat.

It is a criticism that does not bear close examination. To Elizabeth herself, and to most of her principal advisers, the situation appeared differently. It was the accepted opinion throughout England, including Drake in spite of all his eagerness to strike again, that the Cadiz operations had delayed the sailing of the Armada at least until too late in the year to be a reasonably viable venture. To mount a major operation in the English Channel during the winter months, involving the passage of an invading army in barges across normally turbulent waters, was, it was thought, a risk that only a maniac would consider. As the summer gave way to autumn the Privy Council also knew through Burghley's well-spread spy net in Spain that Santa Cruz had not yet returned to Lisbon from his fruitless search for Drake, that the reinforcements from the Mediterranean had still not reached the concentration in Lisbon, and that the Biscayan squadron of Oquendo was still held up at San Lucar awaiting its stores. This intelligence from Spain gave good grounds for the belief that there could be little threat of danger during the remainder of 1587 and that the moment of trial, when it came, must be in 1588.

The average monthly cost of wages and victuals for the main fleet was in the region of £5,000, depending on the number of men on board the ships. It made financial sense to the impecunious Queen to keep the ships in winter quarters without their crews and so save this cost. Drake was still at Plymouth with a squadron of ships in full commission, strong enough to harry the Spaniards in the Channel if the Armada did in fact sail. Another strong squadron under Sir Henry Palmer was based in the stretch of water between the east coast of Kent and the Goodwin Sands, known as the Downs, to blockade Parma in his Netherlands ports in conjunction with a Dutch squadron under Justin of Nassau. This was considered a reasonably stout hedge against the unexpected, and faith in its efficacy avoided the miseries which the Armada was suffering in Lisbon. Winter was the time when ships were docked for repairs and cleaning, and with the crews paid off there was none of the sickness, death, and desertion expected when full crews were living on board. Another advantage was that provisions remained unconsumed and ready for issue when required operationally. But of prime importance was the speed of mobilization which the new professionalism of the Navy had made possible. A fortnight was enough to get the majority of the ships out to sea fully manned and equipped for war. It had been done before on several occasions when danger of attack was anticipated and could be done again, and it was unlikely that the Armada could leave Spain without any knowledge of it reaching England.

It is uncertain exactly when the mobilization of the English fleet was ordered, but evidence points to a date early in January 1588. The commission appointing the Lord High Admiral, Howard of Effingham, as Commander-in-Chief of the fleet was signed by Elizabeth on 31 December 1587. Two days later Drake was appointed to command an independent squadron, based at Plymouth, of thirty ships, to which the Queen contributed seven of her own. The reason for the mobilization was intelligence received from Burghley's spies in Spain that Philip had named 15 February as the date by which the concentration of ships in Lisbon was to be completed, which was taken in London to indicate a sailing date in March, or in April at the very latest. Because of the continuing uncertainty of the actual date of the Armada's sailing, Drake's instructions were to look into the Spanish ports and 'distress' any ships that were assembling in them.

If he found that the Armada was already at sea he was to send the information home in his fastest pinnace and to 'dog' the enemy fleet, attacking whenever he could without undue risk to his own ships.

Before he could get his squadron together, new intelligence reached the Council. A report from the British ambassador in Paris that so great was the sickness, death, and desertion in the Spanish crews that Philip was cancelling the whole of his 'Enterprise of England' was independently confirmed by a similar report from the French King of Navarre. There can be little doubt that this information was deliberately planted by Spain in an attempt to halt the English preparations. Drake never believed it for a moment, neither did Walsingham. We know now that there was no truth in it, but at the time Elizabeth and a majority of the Council accepted it because of the quality of the two independent sources. Elizabeth's immediate reaction was an order to Howard to reduce his crews by one half and to Drake to 'discourage' his taking his squadron to sea but to keep it together in Plymouth.

Hard on the reports from Paris and Navarre came the news from Spain that Santa Cruz was dead. It seemed to the Council in London that the whole Spanish venture was collapsing. The 'discouragement' to Drake was changed to a royal veto to engage in any warlike activity. A Spanish abandonment of the expedition began to look even more probable with a suggestion from Parma that Elizabeth should send commissioners to the Netherlands to talk about peace. They were on their way to discuss possible terms by the beginning of March.

Peace had always been Elizabeth's policy for England. She was one of the staunchest of Protestant rulers and as such prepared always to uphold her faith by any means short of full-scale war. The doctrine of reprisal had given her the means of doing so without the direct involvement of the Crown and she had never hesitated to use it when provoked beyond endurance. Behind all her apparent vacillations of policy during the long imbroglio with Spain lay the knowledge that trade could only flourish in times of peace and that it was only through trade that a nation could become rich and bring employment and contentment to the common people. It was this that she most desired for England. She was not to know that Parma was stringing her peace commissioners along by using every possible delaying tactic until the Armada was on its way from Spain; to Elizabeth it was always a gleam of hope when the other side showed any inclination to talk. Her sometimes bewildering responses in apparently lowering her guard were designed mainly to encourage Spain to back down. But whatever else she was, she was no fool. When Howard and the other senior officers in the fleet asked for leave of absence on the grounds of the continuing peace talks with Parma, she curtly refused their request.

Yet in spite of the negotiations with Parma, the recurring news from Spain of still more active preparations could not be disregarded. The Council met in London at the end of February to decide on the strategy to be adopted to meet the Armada when it came. The plan it came up with was grotesque, a division of the fleet into two powerful squadrons to be based at either end of the English Channel, the eastern under Howard to hold the Narrow Seas off the south-eastern coast, the western under Drake in the seas between Ireland and Spain. If the Armada managed to elude Drake and reach the western end of the Channel, his squadron of about fifty ships was to follow it up the Channel doing as much damage to it as possible, eventually driving it into the hands of Howard and his eastern squadron to continue the good work.

Philip II of Spain, painted by Titian in about 1550. Like his father, Charles V, Philip was a great admirer and patron of Titian and commissioned from him a number of portraits and classical pictures.

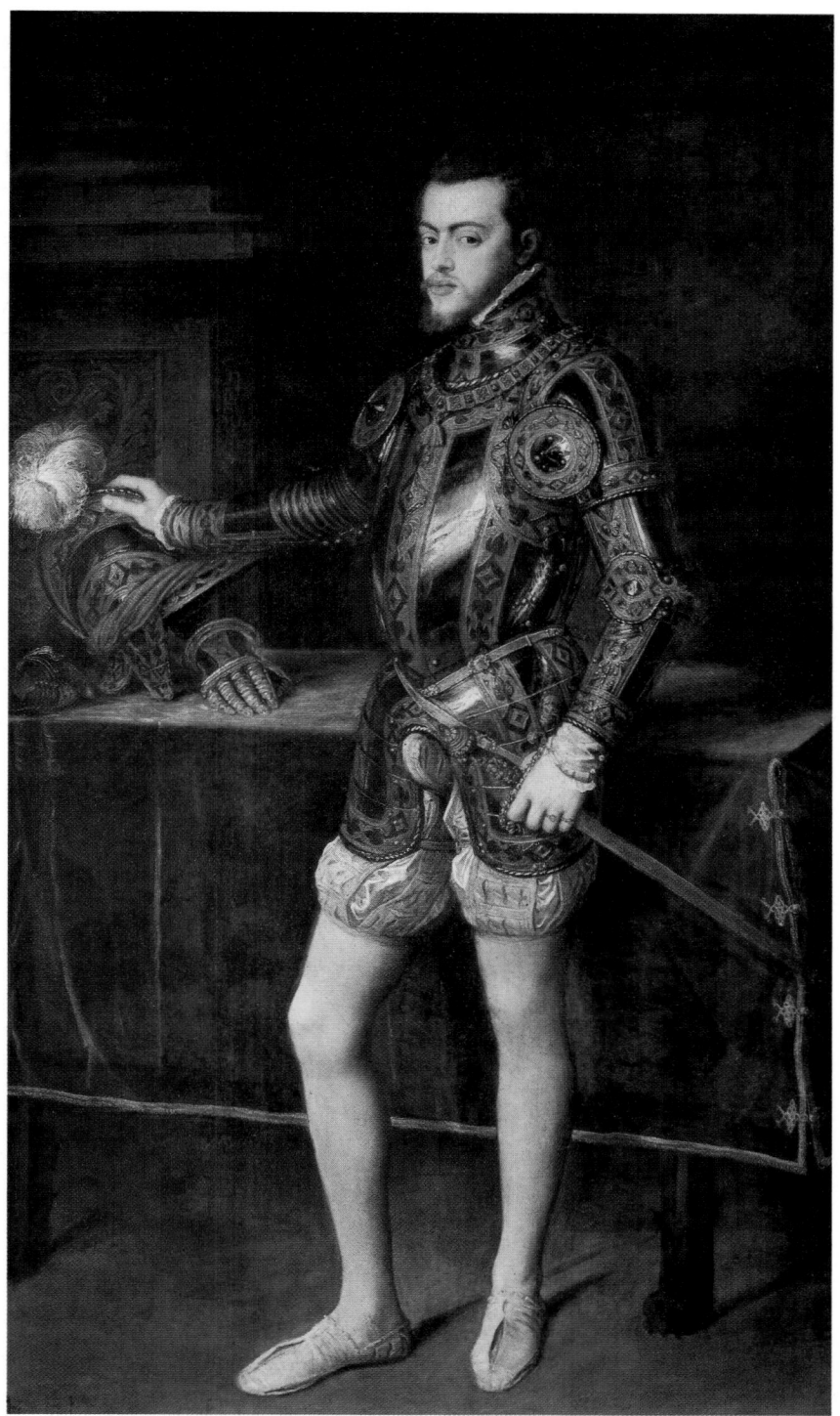

By some means, possibly through Sir James Crofts, Controller of the Household, who did his best to ruin Drake's reputation and good relations with the Queen, Philip learned about this proposed division of the fleet. In his instructions to Medina Sidonia of 1 April he wrote:

> The success of this enterprise depends on your going to the heart of the matter; and even if Drake should have sailed for these waters with a fleet, intending to create a diversion and so embarrass you, as is reported from England, yet you should not turn back, but continue on your course, not seeking out the enemy even if he should remain here. If however he should pursue and overtake you, you may attack him, as you should also do if you meet Drake with his fleet at the entrances to the Channel; because if the enemy's forces are so divided, it would be well to defeat him by stages and thus prevent those forces from uniting.
>
> If you do not encounter the enemy until you reach Margate, and should find there his Admiral of England [Howard] with his fleet alone—or even if he should have united with Drake's fleet, yours will still be superior to both in quality, and also in the cause you are defending, which is God's . . . you may give battle, trying to gain the wind, and all possible advantages from the enemy; and trusting to the Lord to give you victory.

It was entirely due to Drake that this disastrous plan was abandoned in time. He seems to have been the only one among the English naval leaders of the time to appreciate the strategic essentials that this particular situation demanded. He realized that with a divided fleet it would be impossible to deny the enemy command of the sea where and when he most needed it, which was off the coast of Flanders and at Parma's embarkation ports. If the Armada reached there undefeated and unmolested, which it was quite capable of doing if it had only to face half the English fleet at a time, then there would be no possibility of opposing Parma and his army. Drake set out his beliefs in a letter to the Council:

> If her Majesty and your Lordships think that the King of Spain meaneth any invasion of England, then doubtless his force is and will be great in Spain; and thereon he will make his groundwork or foundation, whereby the Prince of Parma may have the better entrance, which in mine own judgment is most to be feared. But if there may be such a stay or stop made by any means of this fleet in Spain, so that they may not come through the seas as conquerors—which I assure myself they think to do—then shall the Prince of Parma have such a check thereby as were meet . . . Good my lords, I beseech you to consider deeply of this [the division of the fleet], for it importeth but the loss of all.

Within four days of the receipt of this letter the Council met again and produced a new plan, though whether as a result of Drake's remonstrations is not known. Howard was now ordered to provide a small reinforcement from his ships for the squadron watching Parma which had been placed under the command of Lord Henry Seymour, with Palmer as his vice-admiral; Howard, meanwhile, was to sail westward with the rest of his fleet to join up with Drake's division at Plymouth. It was the right decision to concentrate the fleet, although any reinforcement of Seymour was quite unnecessary since Parma had no warships of his own and relied entirely on the Armada itself to provide protection for his barges. Howard detached two good ships and a dozen smaller ones for Seymour's reinforcement, the two good ones being the *Rainbow* and the *Vanguard,* both of 500 tons and newly built to the latest design. It is an odd commentary on Tudor naval thought that the sole reason for these two ships being detached was to provide prestigious flagships for Seymour, Howard's nephew, and for Sir William Wynter, who had grown old in the naval service. They might well have contributed much in the coming battles in the west had they been retained in the main fleet instead of being allocated to a useless and unnecessary service.

Although affairs were now moving in the right direction, Drake was still far from satisfied. He believed passionately that the correct strategic place to meet and defeat the Armada was on the coast of Spain at the start of their long voyage to England, and with the whole of the main fleet. He wrote direct to the Queen explaining his concept in detail and Elizabeth summoned him to London to assist the Council. At its meeting he laid out his plans and explained the reasoning behind them. He was opposed by Howard. But Elizabeth, listening intently, was won over. She had always admired Drake, and was captivated by his dash, his forthright opinions, his vigour, which appealed to the adventurous streak in her character. Of all the Tudor monarchs she had proved herself the most courageous when the circumstances demanded a firm lead. And so it was now. With the Queen on his side the opposition to Drake's plans collapsed and Howard was given a free hand to use the fleet as he thought best 'upon such intelligence as he shall receive from time to time'.

On joining Drake at Plymouth Howard presented him with Elizabeth's commission as Vice-Admiral of the fleet, a great and deserved honour. Within a few days he too was won over to Drake's concept of naval strategy. In a letter of 25 June to Walsingham he wrote: 'Sir, you know it hath been the opinion both of her Majesty and others, that it was the surest course to lie on the coast of Spain. I confess my error at that time, which was otherwise. But I did and will yield ever unto them of greater experience.'

Drake, the new Vice-Admiral and the true begetter of the new English naval strategy, had at last come into his own.

7 First Moves

The early summer of 1588 was unusually unsettled with strong and occasionally gale-force winds from the west and south-west alternating with light, variable winds and calms. When Medina Sidonia finally got the Armada to sea from Lisbon on 30 May he ran into a fortnight of variables and calms. So slow was his progress that he decided to put into Corunna, just beyond Cape Finisterre, to refit and revictual. Before he could pass the order to all his ships a sudden change in the weather scattered the Armada as a vicious storm blew up out of the west. Several of the ships had their masts sprung and suffered other storm damage. Many of them eventually found shelter in various harbours along the coast; about twenty others, still unaware of Medina Sidonia's move-ment, continued on their course for the Scilly Islands.

On 24 June Medina Sidonia wrote to Philip urging the abandonment of the inva-sion, a decision with which his council-of-war, with the exception of Pedro de Valdes, had agreed. It was an indication that the majority of Spain's naval leaders had already lost confidence in the face of persistent reports then circulating in Spain of the strength and experience of English sea power.

Predictably, Philip would not hear of it. He sent Medina Sidonia a list of his reasons for continuing the campaign at all costs, pointing out that though some in the Armada might regard the recent storm as a sign from God that Spain was embarking on an unjust war, the reverse was the case. The war in fact was so just that 'no step must therefore be taken by us to interrupt the course of the Divine purpose'. And concerning reports received by Medina Sidonia of the power of the English fleet, he wrote:

> Nor is the enemy's power so great that it could serve as a pretext for us to cease in our pursuit of him; for even though our Armada should remain without some of the missing ships [those that had continued to the Scillies] . . . it is still superior to the fleet which waits for it. Of the enemy's ships, some are old, others small and inferior to ours in strength and general excellence . . . When the tiros in the Armada are mingled with the practical hands, all may be considered as experienced. The enemy's crews, on the other hand, consist of novices, drawn from the common people—a tumultuous crowd lacking military discipline.

In a covering letter enclosing his comments he wrote:

> Duke and Cousin, I have received the letter under your hand of the 24th [June] and from what I know of you, I believe that your bringing all these matters to my attention arises solely from your zeal to serve me . . . stir yourself then to

A pinnace of the Spanish Armada, painted by Cornelis van Wieringen in 1588. The attention to detail is typical of the work of many of the great Dutch marine artists of the period.

The northern coast of Spain, a
chart from the Mariners Mirrour.
The Armada, scattered by a gale
off Cape Finisterre after sailing
from Lisbon, took shelter at
Corunna to repair damage and to
replenish its stores.

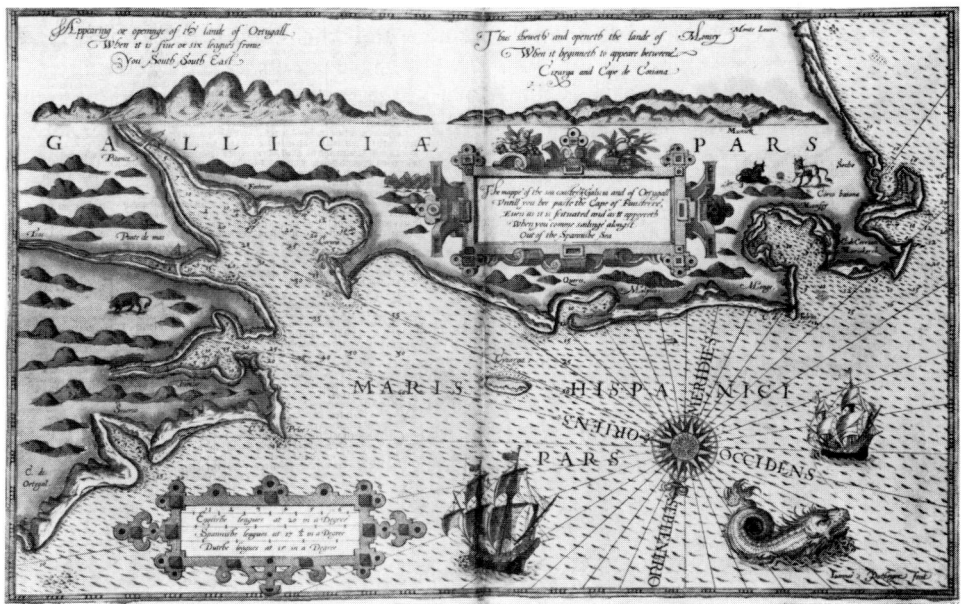

do your duty, since you can see that, pressed as I am by financial and other
difficulties, I am resolute to overcome them all with God's aid . . . Make all ready
with speed so that at the latest you may sail on the 10th of this month [July]
without fail . . . and making do as best you can with the artillery, personnel, and
food which you have now aboard.

When the King commanded there was no alternative for Medina Sidonia but to obey,
in spite of his considerable doubts of the outcome.

Equally unhappy, though for entirely different reasons, were the two English admirals
at Plymouth. With the two original squadrons now forming a single fleet of between
eighty and a hundred ships, and with Howard and Drake at one in believing the Spanish
coast to be the strategically correct place to attack the Armada, there was a hold-up
in the arrival of stores for Howard's squadron of merchant ships contributed by the
City of London. Both men firmly believed that the decision of the Council to give
Howard a free hand to use the fleet as he thought best meant that it approved Drake's
strategy. So it was with considerable consternation that they received contrary orders
on 19 June emanating directly from the Queen. They came in a letter to Howard from
Walsingham instructing him not to go so far south as the coast of Spain but 'to ply
up and down in some indifferent place between the coast of Spain and this realm so
that you may be able to answer any attempt . . . against this realm, Ireland or Scotland.'

Howard, recent recruit though he was to Drake's strategic thought, was at once
up in arms at the absurdity of this new order from the Queen. His resentment was
evident in his letter of reply to Walsingham. He wrote:

But now as by your directions to lie off and on between England and Spain,
the south-west wind that shall bring them to Scotland and Ireland shall put us

to the leeward. The seas are broad; but if we had been on their coast they durst not have put off to have left us on their backs; and when they shall come with the south-westerly wind, which must serve them if they go for Ireland or Scotland, though we be as high as Cape Clear yet shall we not be able to go to them as long as the wind shall be westerly, and if we lie so high then may the Spanish fleet bear with the coast of France to come for the Isle of Wight.

His reasoning was unanswerable and within a few days a letter from the Council restored his liberty of action.

But the ships carrying his provisions continued to be delayed. The squally wind remained firmly in the west holding them up in their passage down the Channel and at the same time penning the fleet in Plymouth. A close search of the surrounding countryside produced sufficient food for about ten days, and, with the wind relenting, Howard put to sea and stood down the Channel on 25 June. But two days later a strong southerly gale blew up and, rather than beat uselessly against it and risk being carried down to leeward of Plymouth, the fleet returned.

Had it been a less vicious storm there could have been a chance of dealing the Armada a blow from which it might not have recovered. The Spanish ships which had failed to observe Medina Sidonia's entry into Corunna reached the rendezvous off the Scillies on about 27 June. They waited there for about a week, expecting the remainder of the Armada to arrive, until a pinnace sent from Corunna reached them and ordered them home. There were some twenty or so of them, all reported as 'great ships' of from 200 to 600 tons, and each with a large red cross emblazoned across its sails. Shots were exchanged with one or two English pinnaces which Drake had sent out to watch for the Armada, but by the time these reached Plymouth to report, the Spanish ships were on their way back to Corunna. Had Howard been able to continue on his course instead of having to battle against the gale, he would certainly have met them, and against a fleet the size of Howard's they would have had no chance.

The southerly gale however brought some good in its train. It broke, even if only temporarily, the sequence of westerly squalls and the lull brought Howard's victuallers at last to Plymouth. Work was started to reprovision his ships, and was in full swing when one of the pinnaces which had seen the Spanish ships off the Scillies came in. Howard's immediate thought was that the Armada had sailed from Spain and that the gale which had driven him back to Plymouth had scattered Medina Sidonia's fleet into groups. He wrote a hurried letter to Walsingham passing on this information and reporting that he expected to be ready for sea early on 5 July. And at last the weather played its part in furthering this hope, with the wind coming fair from the north-east. Without waiting to complete the full revictualling, Howard led the fleet to sea en route to the Scillies on 4 July.

Again the wind played him false. Before he was clear of the Channel it chopped round to south-south-west. There was no chance now of making the Scillies and no other prudent course but to assume that Medina Sidonia had rounded up his scattered ships and was bound for the English Channel. Howard's council-of-war—Drake, Hawkins, Martin Frobisher, and Drake's former flag captain Thomas Fenner—thought it best to await it where they were, and for this purpose the fleet was divided into three, the main body under Howard in the centre, a small squadron of twenty ships under Drake to port and another equally small under Hawkins to starboard. Its purpose was to cover a wider area of sea in a line about one hundred miles long through which the Armada might come.

But still the Armada did not arrive. In its absence Drake became more and more unhappy at Howard's present disposition, protesting that the English fleet had left itself insufficient sea-room to manoeuvre for the wind and that in its present position it could not avoid being to leeward when the Spaniards came. Howard's reply to this was to spread the fleet on a wider front as far out as Ushant. Once again Drake protested. The fact that the Armada had still not been sighted indicated to him that it could not yet have sailed from Spain, and if so, the English ships should be on the Spanish coast, not spread in a line from Cornwall to France.

The fleet was in poor shape when at last the intelligence so desperately needed was received from intercepted merchant ships. Far from sailing to England, the Armada was still at Corunna. The wind again took a hand on 17 July by shifting into the north, a fair wind for Spain. Howard called his council-of-war together again and after much argument, the decision was made to take advantage of the wind and make for Corunna. It was not an easy decision as many of the ships had barely enough provisions on board to reach the Spanish coast, and sickness was spreading though the crews. But it was expected that after the inevitable battle they would be able to make good any shortages from the defeated Spanish ships.

The northerly winds held throughout the night of the 17th and for all of the 18th, and hopes remained high of catching the Armada at a disadvantage. On the 19th, almost within sight of the Spanish coast, the wind began to die out. As the English fleet lay unable to make headway, the wind backed round to the south-west and blew strong and hard. There was no alternative but to turn and run with the wind for Plymouth since, with the crews already on short rations, it was impossible to remain in the hope of yet another change in the wind.

The six weeks in Corunna had not been easy ones for Medina Sidonia. It was nearly a month before the majority of the missing ships came in, and a few never arrived at all. Repairs to the storm-damaged ships went slowly, for the facilities for such work at Corunna were sparse and spare masts and yards to replace those sprung in the gale had to be sought in neighbouring harbours. These however were the least of Medina Sidonia's worries; more serious was the state of his victuals and the casks in which they were stored. In the short passage from Lisbon to Corunna many had leaked and their contents had spoiled. As soon as he learned of the Armada's arrival at Corunna Philip sent one of his secretaries, Andrea da Alba, to consult with Medina Sidonia and gave him *carte blanche* to scour the countryside for all he wanted. Yet even with the casks set up again there was no guarantee that they would survive the longer voyage to England.

Another worry was the sickness which struck at crews. Many men died, others deserted, and some were discharged as no longer of use. Replacements were rounded up in the surrounding countryside, the *tiros* which Philip had mentioned in his earlier letter, but even though Medina Sidonia was no seaman he could recognize that they were useless and likely to become more of a hazard than a help when it came to handling a ship in battle. He got rid of most of them before the Armada finally sailed.

In the face of Philip's constant urging to get to sea Medina Sidonia put as good a face on it as he could. His Armada, as it rested in Corunna, certainly looked impressive.

It was organized in squadrons based territorially on the districts which supplied the ships. Its backbone was the twenty-five galleons belonging to the King, supplemented by forty armed merchant ships, of which most were built on galleon lines with the longer length-to-beam ratio. They were reckoned to be well comparable in fighting power with galleons built purely as warships. But they were poor sailors, as indeed were the royal galleons. Four galleasses and four galleys were included in the fleet. The galleasses were big ships, larger than any others in either fleet, carrying fifty guns and 300 rowers each, in addition to a crew of some 380 soldiers and mariners. There was also a squadron of twenty-three hulks and urcas, ordinary merchant ships not built on galleon lines. Although armed with a total of 384 guns between them they were hardly to be counted as fighting ships as they were heavily laden with extra stores and woefully slow, though they could defend themselves if attacked. The same could be said of a squadron of twenty-two miscellaneous small ships since they too carried guns.

On 19 July Medina Sidonia summoned his Council on board the *San Martin* to consider whether the Armada was ready to put to sea. All his squadron commanders were in favour, even though some of the ships had not fully completed their repairs and most of them were short of trained seamen. Nevertheless, the longer they stayed in Corunna the more the embarked stores would be consumed, and there was no chance of replenishment until they made contact with Parma in the Netherlands. It was best, the Council decided, to sail now. It was full summer, when the prevailing wind could be expected to blow from the south-west, the best wind possible for their task. On the 21st the wind looked settled in this favourable quarter. It was the same wind which had foiled Howard and Drake in their proposed attack on an Armada still at anchor

The Ark Royal, *formerly the* Ark Raleigh *but bought by the Queen from Sir Walter Raleigh for £5,000. Writing to Lord Burghley, Howard of Effingham said of her, 'And I pray you tell her Majesty from me that her money was well given for the Ark Raleigh, for I think her the odd ship in the world for all conditions . . .'*

in Corunna; now it was lifting them home to Plymouth, and the Armada, which sailed out of Corunna on the 21st, followed no more than a couple of days astern of them. The Spanish rendezvous for stragglers on this occasion was no longer the Scilly Islands but Mounts Bay.

The English fleet made a quick passage home and reached Plymouth on 22 July. No time was lost in preparing the ships once again for sea. On the 27th Howard wrote to Walsingham: 'I make all the haste I can possible out; and I and all my company that come from London will not stay for anything.' As always there were sick men to be replaced but even this could not dismay him. 'There shall be neither sickness nor death', he wrote, 'which shall make us yield until this service be ended. I never saw nobler minds than we have here in our forces.'

It was the same spirit everywhere. The letters written to Burghley and Walsingham from the fleet at Plymouth and from Seymour's squadron in the Downs tell the same story, a hymn of confidence and praise for the staunchness of the ships and for the steadfastness of their officers and crews. Even Sir William Wynter, crusty old admiral as he was, could write from the Downs on 28 July: 'Our ships doth show themselves like gallants here. I assure you it will do a man's heart good to behold them; and would to God the Prince of Parma were upon the seas with all his forces and we in view of them . . .' From Plymouth, Howard was equally confident. 'I protest before God,' he wrote to Burghley on 29 July, 'and as my soul shall answer for it, that I think there were never in any place of the world worthier ships than these are for so many. And as few as we are, if the King of Spain's forces be not hundreds, we will make good sport with them.'

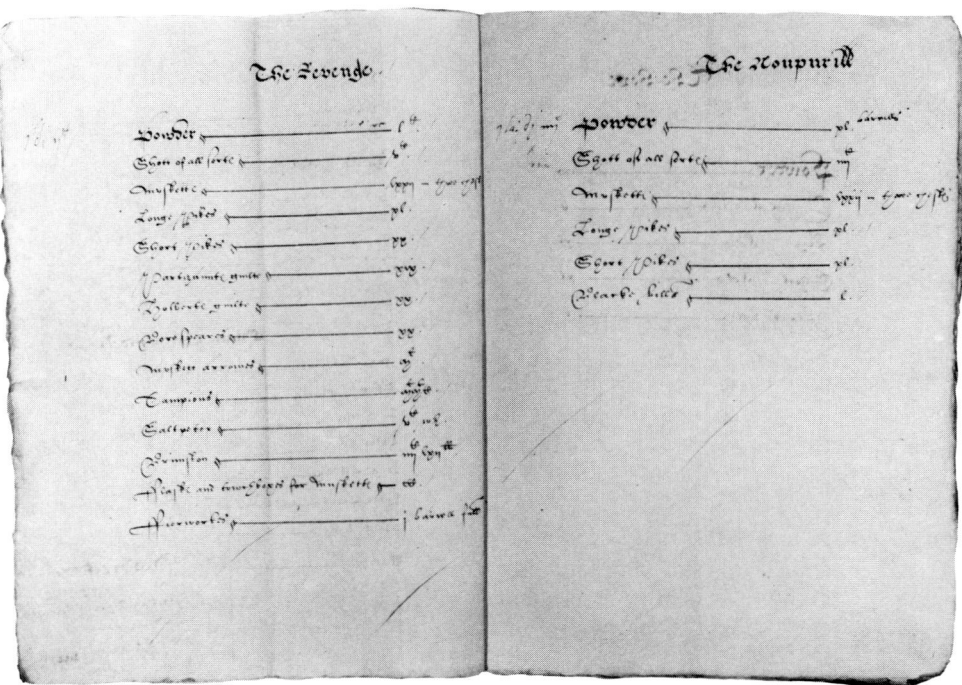

An account of the powder, shot and weapons supplied to the Revenge, *Drake's flagship, and the* Nonpareil, *commanded by Thomas Fenner.*

A bronze cannon cast in 1555, typical of the largest guns mounted in English ships. It bears the arms of Philip of Spain and Mary of England.

Howard's western fleet numbered around one hundred ships, of which sixty-nine were galleons or galleon-built merchant ships, many of them of less than 300 tons. The remainder were pinnaces and small coasters taken up to keep the fighting ships supplied while at sea in the Channel. Howard's junction with Drake at Plymouth was still unknown in Spain; Medina Sidonia expected that the final battle against the main fleet of England under Howard's leadership would be fought in the waters of the southern North Sea, probably between the coasts of Kent and Flanders, and that only Drake with up to about fifty ships would be found guarding the western Channel. His Armada of more than twice that number should guarantee him the victory over even such a formidable opponent as Drake.

It is almost impossible to make a valid comparison between the two fleets engaged in the Channel battles. Clearly there were about twenty-five to thirty more Spanish ships than English during the period of these battles but this possible advantage in numbers was largely neutralized by the higher speed at which the English ships could operate and by the greater range of their guns. On the official figures the aggregate tonnages of the two fleets worked out at about two to one in favour of the Armada but the differences in the methods of tonnage calculation in Spain and England exaggerated the true ratio. The Spanish measurement formula produced tonnages around twenty-five per cent greater in comparison with the English formula and by this amount at least the difference has to be adjusted. As a rough guide, of ships of more than 300 tons the Armada had sixty-two averaging 727 tons, the English fleet twenty-three averaging 552 tons. And of ships between 200 and 300 tons, the Armada had none and the English fleet had twenty-six averaging 210 tons. Again it is difficult to be exact, as these figures apply to all the ships listed in the two fleets and there were some ships on both sides which, for one reason or another, were not present during the Channel battles.

The four galleasses from Naples included in the Armada were in a class apart. They were certainly the largest ships in either fleet but their particular design based on the shallow draught galley form made it impossible to calculate their tonnage under any of the recognized measurement rules. Certainly, ship for ship, the Spanish with their towering castles forward and aft looked considerably larger than the low-charged English ships, and it may be this impression of vast size, remarked by many who were present, that led to the belief so prevalent for centuries that the Armada battles were engagements almost between giants and pigmies. It was nothing so dramatic as that.

It is almost equally impossible to make a comparison between the guns of the two fleets. The actual numbers and types mounted on board varies in the official records of both the English and Spanish fleets and in some of the Spanish ships the gun carriages had no guns to mount on them. The *Rosario*, captured by Drake on the first night

A chart from the Mariners Mirrour *of the western entrance to the English Channel, showing the coast of England from the Sorlings (Scilly Isles) to Plymouth. The Spanish Armada was first sighted and reported as it approached the Lizard.*

in the Channel, was found on examination to have four empty gun carriages. Although on paper the number of Spanish guns was nearly double the number of English, the true proportion was a good deal smaller. In culverins and demi-culverins the English ships were considerably better armed than the Spanish and as the battles between the two fleets went, these were the guns that counted most.

Spanish ship design allowed only for very small gunports to be cut, so small that the muzzle of the gun almost completely filled the space. This put the gunners under a considerable handicap, not only in severely limiting the degree of elevation and training of the guns but also in denying the gunners sight of the ship against which they were firing. This would not have mattered so much had the Spanish ships been fast and weatherly enough to force a close-range action where it was almost impossible to miss, but no Spanish ship in the whole of the Armada had those sailing qualities. It was symptomatic of the Spanish failure to adapt to modern practices, not only in ship design but also in seamanship methods. Almost alone in Europe their ships did not fit the bowline, introduced a few years earlier, which enabled the leeches of the square sails to be sharpened to the wind to produce at least an extra half point in windward performance. It was by no accident that, through all the Armada battles, English ships outsailed and outpointed Spanish ships, a tremendous advantage in action where so much counted on the ability to gain the wind.

In one other aspect the advantage again lay with England, the proportion of sailors and soldiers which made up the crews of the ships. On average, English ships were manned by three sailors to one soldier, Spanish ships by three soldiers to one sailor. This Spanish ascendancy of the military, a legacy of the galley warfare at which Spain had excelled in the Mediterranean, was a fatal handicap in terms of the developing tactics of broadside fire which was the modern method of naval battle. There were not enough mariners in the Spanish crews to handle their ships with that degree of efficiency called for in warfare under sail.

During the afternoon of 29 July Captain Fleming of the *Golden Hind*, who had been sent out to cruise in the western Channel to watch for the Spaniards, reached Plymouth with the information that he had sighted the Armada off the Lizard. Whether Howard and Drake were playing bowls on Plymouth Hoe when Fleming arrived with his news of the Armada, and whether Drake made his famous remark: 'There is time to finish the game and beat the Spaniards too,' must remain romantic conjecture. But whether or no, it makes a good story. There could well have been a game of bowls in progress and Drake would also have known that the flood tide had at least another three hours to run before any English ship could attempt to move out of the harbour in order to meet the approaching Spanish fleet.

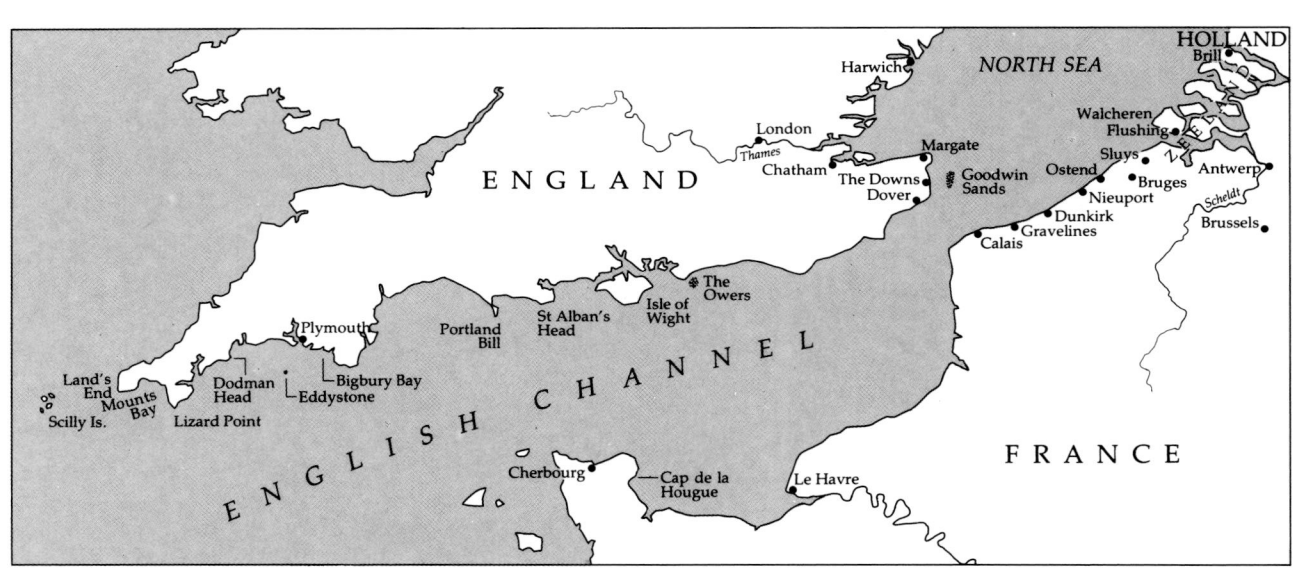

Harwich

London
Thames

NORTH SEA

Chatham

The Downs
Dover

Margate

Goodwin
Sands

ENGLAND

Walcheren
Flushing

Sluys

Ostend

Bruges

Antwerp

Scheldt

Nieuport

Dunkirk

Brussels

Gravelines

Calais

HOLLAND

Brill

The Owers

Isle of
Wight

St Alban's
Head

Portland
Bill

Plymouth

Land's
End
Mounts
Bay

Scilly Is.

Dodman
Head

Eddystone

Bigbury Bay

Lizard Point

ENGLISH CHANNEL

Cherbourg

Cap de la
Hougue

Le Havre

FRANCE

8 The English Channel

The Armada came slowly up from Corunna, held back by the need to adjust its progress to the slow-sailing hulks and urcas. On 27 July, six days after leaving port, it ran into stormy weather in which the four galleys, unable to make headway in the rough seas and unstable by reason of their shallow draught, were forced to seek shelter. One of them, the *Diana*, ran aground at the entrance to Bayonne and was broken up, the other three reached port in safety. Also disabled in the storm was the *Santa Ana*, flagship of Recalde's squadron, though not so badly that she could not later catch up the main body. Until she rejoined, Recalde himself was taken on board the *San Martin*. The storm had scattered the fleet, and in the confusion the Andalusian squadron under Pedro de Valdes, with some twenty or so other ships, had held their course for the fleet rendezvous in Mounts Bay while Medina Sidonia lay to for the scattered ships to reassemble. It was the ships with Valdes that were seen by Captain Fleming and reported to Howard on 29 July.

On the same day Medina Sidonia reached Land's End and waited there, apparently mistaking it for the Lizard. A pinnace was sent in search of Valdes and the missing ships, and on 30 July the Armada was reunited and continued its course up the Channel as far as the Dodman Head. No English ships had yet been sighted and this made it seem likely that they were still in harbour at Plymouth. With the present wind blowing from the south-west they might well be held there, unable to put to sea against a head wind. Medina Sidonia hove to off the Dodman to let any stragglers catch up, ran up to the fore-topmast-head the holy banner that had been blessed in Lisbon Cathedral, and called a council-of-war.

He found himself in the perfect position, the same that Howard and Drake had so hoped to reach a week earlier at Corunna had the wind not changed at the last moment to frustrate them. Down to leeward lay Plymouth. Medina Sidonia still believed that the English ships in harbour there numbered no more than fifty, and the odds would therefore be overwhelming if the whole Armada could attack at once. His pilot and his chart told him that the entrance into Plymouth Sound was narrow and defended by land forts and that he might well lose a ship or two. But only a year earlier Drake had shown how it could be done with his attack at Cadiz where the shore defences and the narrow entrance were at least as formidable as those at Plymouth.

There are conflicting accounts of what was decided at the council-of-war. At first a majority of the squadron commanders, led by the firebrand de Leyva, voted for an immediate attack in order to reap the full advantage of the surprise the Armada had achieved. Medina Sidonia took a more cautious line, wondering how the Armada, if

The English Channel was the open highway through which the ships of northern Europe could reach the oceans of the world. Under the control of Spain, it would bring ruin to the overseas trade of the German states, Holland, France and England.

it succeeded in forcing the entrance to the Sound, could get to sea again if the action against Drake were unsuccessful. Finding it difficult to convince the others, he produced instructions from the King expressly forbidding him to enter any English port until he had made contact with the Duke of Parma. At this point the accounts of the meeting vary. One report holds that the other officers were won round to Medina Sidonia's opinion that to attempt Plymouth was too risky; another that the fleet should continue its course towards Plymouth and attack on arrival if the prospects of success still looked good. After the event Pedro de Valdes wrote to Philip that it was this second course of action which was agreed by the council, and certainly the Armada continued to head towards Plymouth. After he was taken prisoner in the capture of the *Rosario*, Valdes told Drake 'that they thought it would be an easy thing to make themselves masters of Plymouth'. Medina Sidonia, however, in his report to Philip after the Armada's return, wrote that on learning the King's instructions the council had agreed to abandon all thoughts of attack. This may well have been the case, for throughout all the preparations Philip had stressed that the entire operation was God's and that Philip was but His spokesman. To challenge the King's orders might be foolhardy but to challenge God's was blasphemy and in the religious temper of the times was not likely to be risked.

As the Armada approached Plymouth the weather thickened, with drizzle and rain developing. In spite of the limited visibility some ships were sighted ahead but they could not be counted. Even so, they could be nothing but Drake's squadron having by some miracle worked its way against the wind out of the Sound. The sudden change in the situation seems to have caught Medina Sidonia and his advisers undecided on what to do next and the Armada continued slowly on its course. Worse was to follow. An hour or so later one of his pinnaces brought in four prisoners taken from an English fishing boat and for the first time Medina Sidonia learned that Howard had joined Drake and that the ships seen earlier had been their combined squadrons and not Drake's alone as he had originally thought. So he was faced not with fifty ships but more probably one hundred, and the odds in his favour had disappeared. His immediate reaction was to reverse course to seaward to keep the advantage of the wind but Diego Flores de Valdes warned him that the rest of the Armada would be unable to follow him in the dark and that he would find himself with a scattered fleet in the morning. Medina Sidonia decided to anchor for the rest of the night, and sent instructions to his squadron commanders to take up their pre-arranged formation for battle in the morning. It was not the first or the last time that the advice he received from Diego Flores was to lead him into error, for his original thought of keeping the wind by getting to seaward was, in the circumstances, the wisest move he could have made.

During the evening everyone on board the ships saw great volumes of smoke rising from the land; as night fell the view became a forest of twinkling lights. These were the beacons set upon headlands and hills, spreading the message of danger through the length and breadth of the land. It was the signal to call out the train bands, something akin to a territorial army, ostensibly to do battle against the expected invasion but more probably to discourage any thoughts lingering among the English Catholics of rising to assist their co-religionists.

When Captain Fleming brought his news of the Armada to Plymouth during the afternoon of 29 July the tide was flooding. It would need to reach high water and turn

A map of the beacons of Kent, from Lombard's Perambulation of Kent. *Beacons were lit to spread the warning that the Spanish Armada had arrived in the English Channel.*

to the ebb before the English ships could begin to move. Everyone in Plymouth could see where the danger lay and that the only possible way to meet it was to get the ships out to sea as quickly as possible. As the tide reached its height and turned, work went on throughout the night to warp as many ships as possible out of the harbour and into the Sound. During the morning of the 30th they began to beat out of the Sound against a wind still blowing steadily from the south-west. This was the moment when Hawkins's new hull design proved its excellence, in a feat of seamanship which the Spanish admirals, still holding their council-of-war on board the *San Martin*, considered impossible. No ship was lost, no ship ran aground, and by the afternoon Howard was at sea in the vicinity of the Eddystone Rock with fifty-four ships in company. The Armada was in sight of them some fifteen miles to windward. The early drizzle turned to rain, and with the wind dropping away there was no more to be done except lie to under bare poles and wait for the wind to pick up again.

It came with the rising of the moon and, making sail, Howard led the fleet southward, close-hauled on the starboard tack, across the front of the Armada. During the early evening another eight ships had come successfully out of Plymouth and, too late to join Howard, were working westward in short tacks under the land and to leeward of the Armada. This movement was closely observed by the Spaniards and it may well be that by directing all their attention towards this small squadron they failed to observe Howard with the bulk of the English fleet crossing ahead of them. During the night the wind veered towards the west, enabling Howard to edge more westerly and to gain that great prize of battle during the sailing ship era, the windward gauge of the enemy.

At dawn on 31 July the English fleet was some six miles to the west of the Eddystone, with the Armada in its order of battle almost precisely to leeward. To the English

The first of the battles off Plymouth, an engraving by Augustine Ryther from a chart drawn by Robert Adams (published 1590). It shows the ships of Howard and Drake emerging from Plymouth and sailing close-hauled to the south, while a smaller group of ships tacks inshore of the Armada to reach a position to windward of the Spanish fleet.

the Armada appeared to be a great crescent of ships, but this impression was probably caused by the wing squadrons of Recalde and Bertendona spread to port and starboard of the rear division, with the two squadrons of royal galleons leading the van and the hulks clustered astern of them.

With the coming of daylight Howard's ships went about onto the port tack, and the first sight the Spaniards had of them was in the last place they expected to see them, to windward and bearing down on the Armada in line ahead, with their guns run out. At the same time the small English squadron that they had been watching through the night finally weathered the Spaniards' port flank and streamed down to join the rest of the English fleet. In the space of little more than twelve hours Medina Sidonia had lost his position of overwhelming surprise and advantage. He had lost, too, if he had ever meant to seize it, the chance of inflicting a crushing defeat on an enemy which he thought he had at his mercy. He had also learned something else that must have filled him with foreboding. To reach the position in which they had been discovered when daylight arrived that morning, English ships had achieved something beyond the capacity of Spanish ships, the ability to hold a course closer to the wind and secure for themselves the pre-eminent position in all naval battle. The Spanish battle tactics were geared to the practice of attack and capture by boarding; the speed and agility of English ships which he had just witnessed made it almost impossible for any Spanish ships to get close enough to exercise the action necessary for subsequent boarding. Whatever hopes of ultimate success he may have had must have begun to fade at that moment.

There was a small traditional ceremony to be observed before battle was joined, the offering of 'defiance' to the Spanish admiral as an invitation to fight. Howard sent one of his pinnaces, the *Disdain*, forward towards the *San Martin* to discharge her small guns at her and, this formality over, led the fleet in line ahead to engage the weather wing of the Armada. The Spanish ships began to give way before the rapidity of the English gunfire, and in an attempt to stop the movement Recalde in the *Santa Ana* came up into the wind to receive the brunt of the English attack. For nearly two hours his ship battled it out virtually alone until the *Gran Grin*, one of the three largest galleons in the Armada, managed to work her way to windward to Recalde's assistance. The *San Martin* and *San Mateo* were also on their way and as they came up they were engaged by the majority of the English ships, a concentration of fire of many upon the few. By this time most of the Armada was working to windward and Howard flew the signal to disengage. He did not wish to risk a general engagement at this point as he was still waiting for the rest of the fleet, another twenty to thirty ships, to make their way out of Plymouth and join him at sea. Besides, Plymouth was now safe from attack, for as a result of the morning's engagement the Armada was now to leeward of the port.

The English, still in their windward position, watched the Armada re-form, and Howard took this opportunity to write to Walsingham about the day's fighting:

> At nine of the clock we gave them fight which continued until one. In this fight we made some of them bear room [forced them to leeward] to stop their leaks, notwithstanding we durst not adventure to put in among them, their fleet being so strong . . . Sir, the captains in her Majesty's ships have behaved themselves most bravely and like men hitherto, and I doubt not will continue, to their great commendation.

As the English fleet lay to and watched the movement of the Armada, an explosion was seen in one of the largest Spanish ships and her stern was engulfed in flames. She was the *San Salvador* of 958 (Spanish) tons and carried on board the paymaster-general of the Armada with his chests of ducats. According to some Spanish sources the explosion was caused by one of her gunners throwing the smouldering end of his slow-match into an open cask of gunpowder. He had been savagely thrashed by one of the military officers of the ship for having his wife on board and, assuming that the officer intended taking the lady for himself, took this grisly revenge. Whatever the cause, the *San Salvador* began to drift astern and Howard, seeing the chance of finishing her off, made sail towards her, the rest of the fleet following. Medina Sidonia, too, saw her plight and bore up to her assistance. Recalde, unable to defend himself in the *Santa Ana* after the battering he had taken earlier and seeing the English ships approaching, also called for assistance, bringing more Spanish ships to the scene. For a time it looked as though the two fleets might again be in action, until Howard withdrew. Later that night the *San Salvador* was abandoned and she was picked up next morning by Howard who sent her in to Weymouth as a prize.

The response to Recalde's call for assistance resulted in another Spanish casualty. In his eagerness to reach the scene Pedro de Valdes ran his ship, the *Rosario*, into the *Santa Catalina* and sheared off his bowsprit. The consequent loss of forestay and fore-topmast stay eventually brought down the foremast which fouled the mainmast as it fell. Unable to make any way through the water, she fell astern. Medina Sidonia ordered a galleasse and a galleon to try to take her in tow and brought the *San Martin* down to stand by her while the attempt was made. It was late evening and the light was beginning to fail. Diego Flores de Valdes, who disliked his cousin Pedro, remonstrated with the Commander-in-Chief, pointing out that his duty was with the Armada as a whole and not with one disabled ship. As a result, Medina Sidonia resumed his place in the van of the Armada, leaving the galleasse and the galleon with the *Rosario*. But as darkness fell the two ships rejoined the Armada, leaving Pedro de Valdes to fend for himself, his ship stationary in the water.

On 31 July, at a council-of-war called by Howard in the *Ark* it was thought that, having failed to attack Plymouth, Medina Sidonia's next objective would be either Portland or the Isle of Wight. Both offered good anchorage sheltered from the prevailing winds and either would provide him with an advanced base in the English Channel. The council therefore decided that the best response would be to continue the chase of the Armada as soon as the remaining ships had joined the fleet from Plymouth, and then to try to drive it on down the Channel. Seymour and his forty ships were waiting in the Downs and their added strength, should the Armada be forced into the eastern end of the Channel, might well be decisive in the final battle. Howard gave Drake the honour of leading the fleet through the night, as a mark of respect for his greater experience in fighting the Spaniards. At midnight the English fleet, with a light burning in the poop-lantern of Drake's ship the *Revenge*, made sail in the wake of the Armada.

During the night the guiding light in the *Revenge* was suddenly extinguished. Howard, next astern of Drake, continued on the course as best he could and at last discovered a faint light ahead of him. Two other ships, the *Bear* and the *Mary Rose*, remained with him; the rest of the ships' captains shortened sail or hove-to until daylight should make all clear.

According to Drake's explanation of the night's events, he had sighted early in the morning three or four ships steering west and thought they might be Spaniards trying to work to windward. Not wishing to lead the fleet away from the main body of the Armada he had extinguished his light and, with the *Roebuck* in company, had gone to investigate. The ships turned out to be German merchantmen, but as he was leaving them he sighted another ship stopped in the water. She was the *Rosario* and he took her without a fight. She proved to be a remarkably rich prize. Pedro de Valdes was on board and he and his entourage became Drake's prisoners in the *Revenge*, bringing with them 55,000 gold ducats. Drake sent the *Rosario* into Torbay, escorted by the *Roebuck*. Pedro de Valdes remained Drake's prisoner for another three years until his family in Spain raised £3,000 to ransom him.

Drake was already a rich man and had no need to augment his considerable fortune. Perhaps the kindest explanation of his conduct that night is to suggest that, for a moment, Drake the corsair usurped the position of Drake the Vice-Admiral and that the habits of a lifetime proved stronger than the duty of leading the fleet which Howard had given him. But however one looks at it, there can be no doubt that it was Drake who was directly responsible for the mess in which the English fleet found itself the next morning.

As dawn broke on 1 August Howard discovered that the light he had been following in the darkness belonged to the Armada and that the *Ark*, *Bear* and *Mary Rose* were within culverin shot of the enemy, with the rest of the English fleet hull down

'La Armada Invencible', *painted by Cornelisz Vroom. The two ships firing at each other in the foreground illustrate the widely held impression that the Spanish vessels were considerably larger than the English.*

The Spanish galleon N.S. del Rosario, damaged in the battle off Plymouth, is captured by Drake. This somewhat imaginative picture is an engraving by John Pine of one of the Armada tapestries made for Howard of Effingham from designs by Cornelisz Vroom.

on the western horizon. There was no danger in this position as they were still to windward, but it meant a wasted day as Howard waited for the ships astern of him to come up and re-form. In the evening the wind dropped to a flat calm and the two fleets lay motionless less than two miles apart in the stretch of the Channel between St. Alban's Head and Portland Bill.

Yet the day was not entirely barren, though not through any action by the English. The adventitious loss of two of their best ships had dispirited the men of the Armada. Alonso Vañegas, a captain on board the *San Martin*, wrote: 'The desertion of the ship that had blown up [*San Salvador*] and the loss of Don Pedro de Valdes, shook the spirit of the people. From that time forward there was no real heart in them.' Another Spanish captain wrote: 'These misfortunes presaged our failure. The evil omen depressed the whole Armada.' But the true unease went deeper than that, a recognition that ran throughout the whole Armada that the new English galleon design had frustrated the only means of Spanish victory, close action and boarding. All their Mediterranean successes had taught them that; all their ships were designed and armed and manned to that purpose. It was no wonder that 'from that time forward there was no real heart in them'.

At sunrise on 2 August the wind came in from the north-east and for the first time the Armada had the weather advantage and the chance of forcing on the English ships the type of warfare they needed. As the wind rose Howard led northward in an attempt to gain the wind, but Medina Sidonia observed the move and led his galleons on a parallel course. The four galleasses were ahead of him on their way towards a group of six English ships, separated from the main fleet. They were the *Triumph*, with

Frobisher on board, and five of the large London merchant ships, and it was apparent to Spanish and English alike that they were in a position of considerable danger.

When Howard saw that his move to the north was being matched by Medina Sidonia, he tacked onto an easterly course, in an attempt to weather the Spanish rear. His change of course was seen by de Leyva in the Spanish rear, who brought his squadron down in line abreast, hoping to force a close action and subsequent boarding of Howard's ships. The gun battle was so fierce that de Leyva had to give way, but as Howard drew clear the Spanish ships closed the gap behind him and virtually cut him and his ships off from the rest of the fleet. Howard bore away to seaward but was unable to shake off de Leyva and his pursuing ships.

Howard was now in danger and for a time it looked as though he could not escape. But as the morning wore on the wind began to veer, first to south-east and then to south-south-west, and this shift in direction brought relief to the English. It gave Howard the ability to win free from de Leyva and at the same time brought a group of some fifty English ships, led by Hawkins and Drake, to windward of the Armada. They threatened the seaward wing of the Spanish fleet and by the fury of their attack forced it down to leeward. As a result of all these moves the Armada had become widely scattered, and Medina Sidonia was forced to re-form its defensive formation. He did so by concentrating the squadrons on his landward wing, which preserved his chances of finishing off Frobisher and his six ships, which were still isolated and now hotly engaged by the galleasses.

Frobisher's position was changing fast. The shift in the wind had put him to leeward of the English fleet and the way was open to English ships to come to his rescue. Howard saw the chance and led off in the *Ark*, followed by the *Elizabeth Jonas, Galleon Leicester, Golden Lion, Victory, Mary Rose, Dreadnought* and *Swallow*, a force of sufficient power to drive off the galleasses. Medina Sidonia led his squadron down to intercept the *Ark* and once again Howard and his ships were cut off from the rest of the fleet. But Medina Sidonia's move was interrupted by a call for help from Recalde, whose flagship had been isolated in Drake's and Hawkins's attack. Medina Sidonia ordered the rest of his squadron to Recalde's rescue, though holding his course in the *San Martin* towards the prize of capturing Frobisher's six ships. As he did so Howard changed course and led his ships direct towards the *San Martin*, now on her own. As they passed they poured their broadside fire into her. Drake, too, took a hand in this action. As Medina Sidonia's galleons came up to relieve Recalde in the *Santa Ana*, he called his ships off to join the attack on the *San Martin*. His arrival freed Howard to return to his original intention. As he approached, the four great galleasses made off, enabling Frobisher's ships to rejoin the English fleet.

It had been a day of confused fighting, with little credit to either side. The four Spanish galleasses should certainly have taken the English ships. With three hundred rowers in each ship they were independent of the wind, and with two hundred guns between them they had enough gun power to break Frobisher's stubborn resistance. It seems that the captain-general of the galleasses, Don Hugo de Monçada, a Catalan knight of great seniority, had taken offence when Medina Sidonia had refused him permission to attack the English Commander-in-Chief, reserving that honour for himself, and had failed to obey Medina Sidonia's instructions when the six ships had been observed separated from the remainder of the English fleet. On such small things can hang the difference between success and failure. For the rest, we have the report from

The Armada under attack during its passage up Channel. In the foreground two English galleons are engaged with a Spanish galleasse. The ship on the right is the Ark Royal, Howard of Effingham's *flagship.*

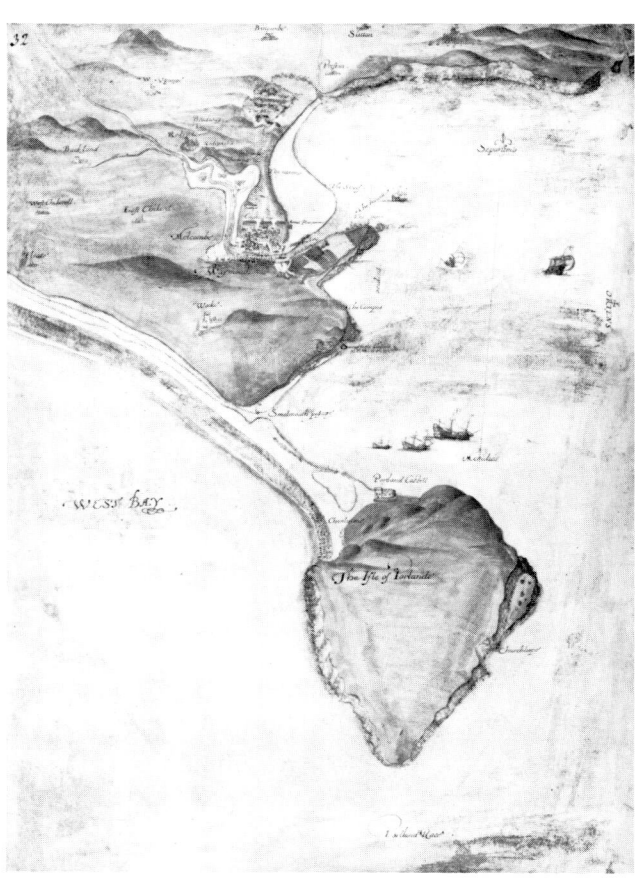

Portland Bill and Weymouth, a contemporary map. The English admirals were concerned that Medina Sidonia would capture Portland and use the anchorage protected by the Chesil Bank as a place of shelter and replenishment.

Don Luis Vañegas, a captain on Medina Sidonia's staff, that the attack on the *San Martin* had cost fifty men killed and sixty men wounded and that her rigging had been badly cut about, though she was by no means put out of action as a fighting ship. The *Santa Ana*, Recalde's flagship, was once again severely damaged but could be temporarily repaired. As the day ended and the Armada continued on its course up the Channel in its close defensive formation, it was still a most formidable force. The English fleet had suffered little damage but it had not fought as a cohesive whole. It had been split up into three groups during the day's action, each one fighting independently of the other two. And this was no way to fight against so well organized and disciplined a fleet as the Armada.

Howard and his admirals were quick to see where the trouble lay. They could not fail to admire the squadronal division of the Armada or to recognize the flexibility it gave Medina Sidonia in adjusting his fleet formation to the changing fortunes of battle and of using squadrons independently when the need arose. At the council-of-war held on board the *Ark* that evening it was decided to re-form the fleet into four squadrons, each under the command of its own admiral, and to divide the new ships, as they arrived daily from the Channel ports to join the fleet, equally between the

four divisions. The new ships were all merchantmen, unused to the necessary discipline of a fleet, and they needed to be placed under experienced naval leaders if they were to be of any value. The four squadrons were disposed abreast of each other, with Frobisher's on the port wing and Drake's on the starboard, Howard's and Hawkins's in the centre. The existence of four squadrons would enable the fleet to attack the Armada in four different places simultaneously. The council also put forward a plan for six merchant ships from each squadron to make simultaneous night attacks in different sectors in order to loosen the Armada's defensive formation, in preparation for a concentrated attack by the whole fleet during daylight. This plan was not carried out as the wind dropped away at dusk and both fleets lay becalmed.

On his arrival at the entrance to the Channel on 29 July Medina Sidonia had proposed, and his council had agreed, that the Armada should wait at the Isle of Wight until a reply was received from Parma fixing a time and place for the meeting of the sea and land forces for the invasion. His pilots had pointed out to him the dangers of lying with his ships off the exposed Flemish coast, with its maze of sandbanks and its lack of a deep-water port to provide adequate shelter. It made sense, therefore, to do the waiting at the Isle of Wight which provided an anchorage well sheltered

Alexander Farnese, Duke of Parma, a portrait by Otto van Veen. Parma and his army of 30,000 soldiers were to be escorted by the Armada across the Channel from Flanders to Kent and mount the invasion of England.

The progress of the Armada up Channel following the battle of Portland, an engraving by Augustine Ryther of a chart drawn by Robert Adams. On the left Howard attempts to relieve Frobisher's ships which have been isolated by the Spaniards; on the right the English fleet has been reorganized into four squadrons.

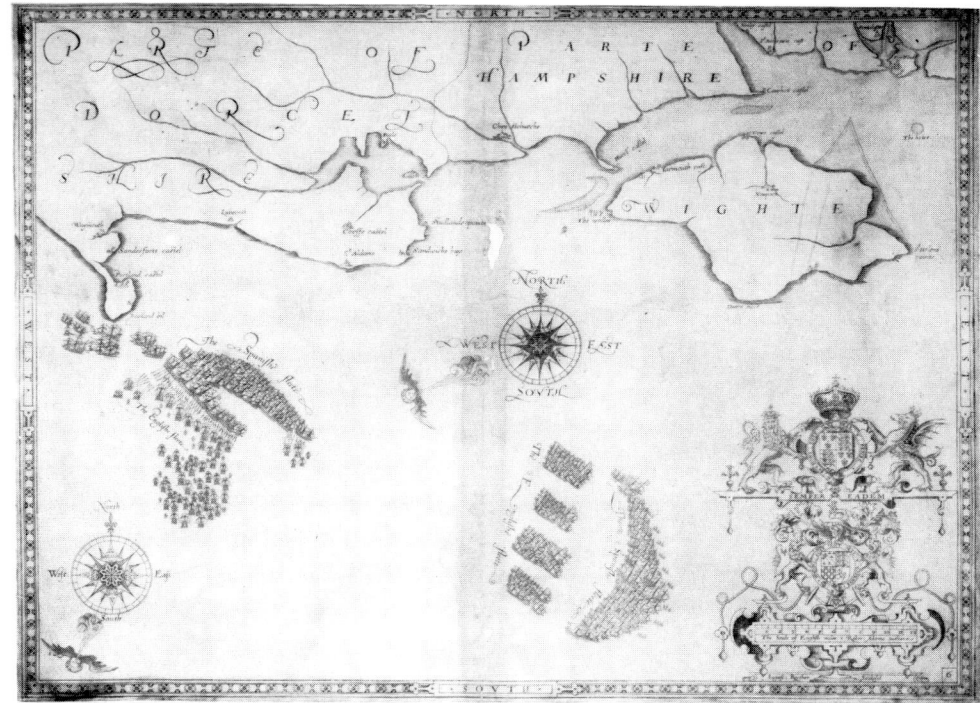

from the prevailing winds. He had kept Parma fully informed of the Armada's progress since leaving Corunna, from time to time sending an officer in a pinnace to the French coast, to make his way overland to Parma's headquarters at Bruges. He sent his intention of waiting at the Isle of Wight to Parma by the hand of Captain Rodrigo Tello, but no reply had been forthcoming. With time running short and his arrival at the Isle of Wight little more than three or four days away, he appears to have changed his plan, for on 31 July, after the fighting off Plymouth, he sent his ensign-bearer, Juan Gil, with another message to Parma, saying that he would make for Dunkirk and begging Parma to have his army and all its stores embarked by the time of his arrival since the Armada could not remain waiting off an exposed coast.

Two days later, after the engagement off Portland and with still no word from Parma, he sent off Captain Pedro de Leon with a similar message. He must have begun to wonder what lay behind the protracted silence since as long ago as February Parma had reported to Philip that he and his army were ready and only waiting for the Armada to arrive. Perhaps another consideration leading to his abandonment of the Isle of Wight as a temporary anchorage was his surprise at the size of the English fleet, which would be able to pick off his ships one by one as they lay at anchor while he was forced to wait for news from Parma.

The Isle of Wight was also looming large in Howard's thoughts. He saw it as a possible, even a probable, target for the Armada and thought that Medina Sidonia might try to occupy it as a jumping-off ground for the invasion. Although his fleet was still intact and growing daily in size, he was concerned that so far he had been

Opposite: Lord Howard of Effingham, painted by Daniel Mytens. He held the office of Lord High Admiral of England in 1588 and commanded the fleet during the battles fought against the Spanish Armada.

unable to stop the Armada's progress or to do any serious damage to its ships. A Spanish occupation of the Isle of Wight would present England with serious problems and stretch her defences to the utmost, particularly if Parma managed to break loose from Seymour in the east. As he saw it, his immediate task was to keep the Armada on the move at all costs.

On 3 August there was so little wind that there as no chance of bringing the Armada again to battle. There was a small brush when the Spanish *Gran Grifon*, escorting the hulks, fell astern and was engaged by Drake's squadron, but Howard broke off the action to conserve ammunition until fresh supplies could reach him from the shore.

By 4 August the Isle of Wight was in sight. The wind was very light at dawn and what little there was came out of the south, slightly favouring the Armada should it freshen. The day's action began with the *Santa Ana* dropping astern of her squadron. She had been until now Recalde's flagship but had been so badly damaged in the previous fighting that he transferred his flag into the *San Juan* of Medina Sidonia's squadron. The *Santa Ana* was engaged by two or three of the rearmost ships of Hawkins's squadron, using their ships' boats to tow themselves within range. To the *Santa Ana*'s rescue came three of the galleasses and de Leyva in the *Rata*, to be met by Howard in the *Ark* and Lord Thomas Howard in the *Golden Lion*. Howard's account of the morning's fight relates how the English ships:

> . . . fought a long time and much damaged them, that one of them was fain to be carried away upon the careen [listing heavily], and another, by a shot from the *Ark*, lost her lantern which came swimming by, and the third his nose [beakhead]. There were many good shots made by the *Ark* and the *Lion* at the galleasses in the sight of both armies [navies], which looked on and could not approach, it being calm, for the *Ark* and *Lion* did tow to the galleasses with their long boats. At length it began to blow a little gale, and the Spanish fleet edged up to succour their galleasses, and so rescued them and the galleon, after which time the galleasses were never seen in fight any more, so bad was their entertainment in this encounter.

The ship seen to be retiring on the careen was the *Santa Ana*. She had again been heavily damaged, so much so that she was unable to keep her station in the Spanish fleet. During the night she drifted away to La Hougue on the French coast, and from there to Le Havre, where eventually she became a total wreck.

Meanwhile Frobisher was again in trouble. He had attempted to attack the port or northernmost wing of the Armada but the wind was so light that he had difficulty in getting clear after a brief action in which the *Triumph* had received some damage. Vañegas, describing this part of the battle, wrote:

> His admiral [*Triumph*], being much damaged, drove a little to leeward of our fleet. Our flagship cast a boat [was towed] towards her . . . and all the other ships of our Armada [the rest of Medina Sidonia's squadron]; while the enemy's ships recovered the wind and guarded their flagship, which was so mauled in the action that she struck her standard and fired guns as signals of distress, and was at length towed by eleven of the enemy's longboats. Our flagship [*San Martin*] and the second in command, and the rest of the ships gained on her so much that the enemy drew close about her to support her, it appearing certain that we would

that day succeed in boarding her, that being the only way to victory. But at that moment the wind freshened in favour of the enemy's admiral and she began to slip away from us.

According to both Howard and Medina Sidonia, that was the end of the day's fighting. As the account taken from Medina Sidonia's *Relation* (compiled by his staff) has it: 'The Duke, seeing that in the intended attack [on the *Triumph*] the advantage would no longer be with us, fired a gun and proceeded on his course, the rest of the Armada following in very good order, and the enemy remaining far astern.' It is here that some doubt arises. Some recent historians describe how Drake and Hawkins led an attack on the starboard wing of the Armada and drove it northward until the whole Spanish fleet was in danger of being stranded on the Owers, the shallow banks to the east of the Isle of Wight. It was this danger, they suggest, that forced Medina Sidonia to abandon his intention of remaining there. Their description is based on an account written by the master of a ship in the Seville squadron which seems to bear it out. The enemy, he wrote, 'charged upon the said wing, in such wise that we who were there were driven into a corner, so that if the duke had not gone about with his flagship, instead of conquerors that we were, we should have come out vanquished that day.'

We know that Medina Sidonia had already abandoned his intention to remain at the Isle of Wight, so it cannot have been this attack which drove him forward. It is surprising, too, that Drake himself does not mention such an attack. Some little time after the campaign Petruccio Ubaldino, a Florentine historian living in England, wrote an account of the Armada battles from information given him by Drake. Ubaldino dates his account as 15 April 1589 so that Drake's memory of the event should still have been fresh. There remains a question mark relating to the events of that battle.

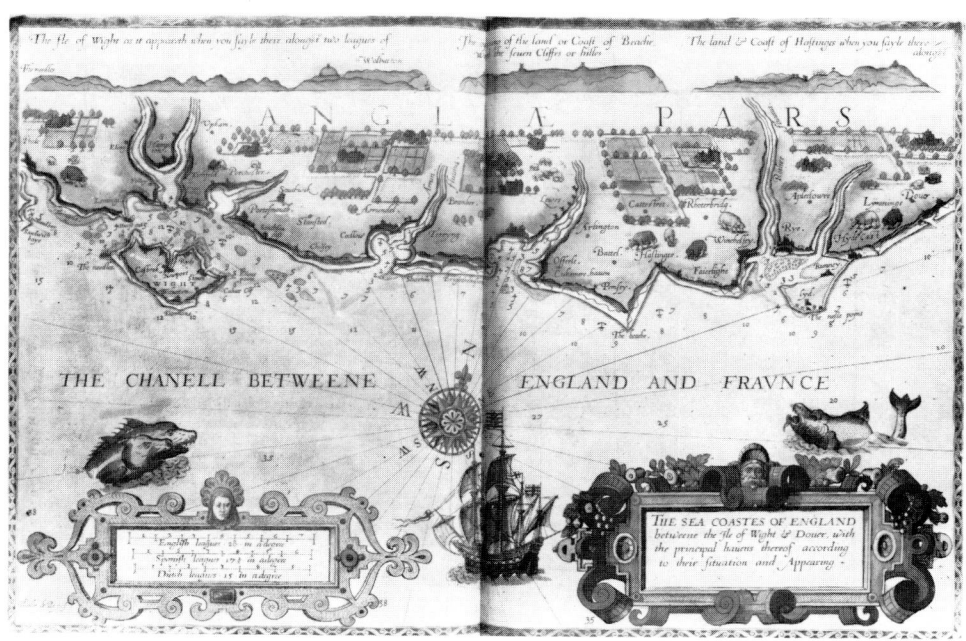

The English Channel coast from the Isle of Wight to Dover, a chart from the Mariners Mirrour. *The last of the battles fought within the English Channel was off the Isle of Wight. At one time the Spanish considered capturing the island as the jumping-off point for the invasion by Parma's army.*

Medina Sidonia was now running short of ammunition. That evening he sent Domingo Ochoa, one of his pilots, with another message to Parma asking for '4 lb., 6 lb., and 10 lb. shot because much of his munition had been expended in the successive fight'. The pilot, he added:

> . . . was also to inform the duke that it would be well for him to be ready to come out and join the Armada when it should arrive in sight of Dunquerque. Thither the Duke of Medina Sidonia was proceeding cautiously, fearing that Parma might not be there seeing that Don Rodrigo Tello had not returned nor had any other messenger come thence.

As a precaution against an unprepared Parma, Medina Sidonia decided to make first for a French port. He knew that France, with the Duke of Guise now controlling Paris, had guaranteed neutrality in Philip's 'Enterprise of England' and that in a French port he would be able to replenish his victuals and fresh water, both of which were running short. He might also be able to buy more shot for his guns. So he set a course for Calais, near enough to Dunkirk to pick up Parma when he was ready and, he hoped, receptive to his need for supplies.

As the Armada, in its defensive formation, shaped course towards the east, Howard followed. He took the occasion to call on board the *Ark* those who had particularly distinguished themselves in the fighting so far. As Lord High Admiral he had the right to reward valour with a knighthood and he knighted John Hawkins, Martin Frobisher, Lord Thomas Howard, Lord Sheffield, Roger Townshend and George Beeston, captain of the *Dreadnought*. As the ceremony ended a French ship from Le Havre approached the fleet bringing the latest 'news' from Europe. Howard and the new knights learned to their surprise of a Spanish victory so great and decisive that the entire English fleet had been scattered, with heavy losses in ships and men. This story was possibly fabricated and certainly circulated by Spanish agents. Howard also learned that, in spite of the Duke of Guise, France was remaining neutral and would not rise in support of Spain. At least that piece of information was welcome, as it had been one of Howard's worries that Guise co-operation with the Armada might set at nought all the English hopes of success in resisting a Spanish invasion.

During the next day the weather worsened with a squally wind from the southwest. The Armada held its course, with the four columns of the English fleet no more than a mile astern of it. In the evening Calais was in sight. As the Spanish anchors brought the Armada to a halt under the cliffs of Calais, English anchors did the same for the English fleet. It was still dead to windward of the Armada and less than a culverin shot away.

Sir Martin Frobisher, painted by Cornelius Ketel. Better known perhaps for his voyages in search of the North-West Passage, Frobisher was an impetuous if gallant admiral and he frequently led his ships into situations of great danger.

9 Gravelines

By his good judgement throughout the Channel battles, Howard had achieved the first of his responsibilities by denying the Armada both time and opportunity to land and occupy any part of England. He and his fleet had harried it throughout its passage up the Channel, always at its heels, always driving it to leeward of every possible anchorage or landing place. Now it was anchored off a French port and the next essential task was clear. He must deny it time to revictual its ships and replenish their ammunition, and drive it out to sea before it could make contact with Parma's army of invasion.

Medina Sidonia, too, had some good grounds for optimism. Although he had lost three of his best ships, the Armada was still in good shape; he could reasonably expect some co-operation from the French in restocking his ships; he was no more than twenty miles from Dunkirk; and if Parma was as good as his word, his army should be embarked in its barges by the time the Armada reached the rendezvous. Almost as he anchored he sent off two messengers. The first was Captain Heredia, who went to the French governor of the port, assuring him that the Armada offered no threat to French sovereignty and asking for help in supplying provisions. The second was Secretary Arçao, who was sent to Parma to inform him of the Armada's arrival at Calais and that it could not delay there without imperilling the ships. Captain Heredia was soon back on board with the governor's promise of assistance apart from ammunition, of which he had none to spare.

Later that evening there was an ominous sign: 'This evening,' wrote Medina Sidonia, 'thirty-six ships joined the enemy, whereof five were huge galleons. This was supposed to be the squadron which Juan Acles had under his charge before Dunquerque. They all anchored about a league from our Armada.' Juan Acles was the name by which John Hawkins was known in Spain, but it was of course not Hawkins but Seymour, with his squadron from the Downs. With their arrival, the strength of the English fleet rose to around 140 ships. One of the Spanish captains counted it as 136, but at no time during the whole campaign is it possible to be sure of the exact numbers present in either fleet.

Early next morning the worst possible news reached the Armada. Don Rodrigo Tello, Medina Sidonia's messenger to Parma when he first reached the English Channel, returned from Dunkirk. He reported that Parma was still at his headquarters at Bruges and that at Dunkirk neither men nor stores were being embarked in the barges. This was confirmed later the same day when Secretary Arçao returned and reported that in his opinion it was impossible for the army to be ready for the invasion in less than a fortnight.

A contemporary drawing of Calais showing its fortifications and the inner harbour. The Armada anchored in the roads, to the left of the harbour, with the English fleet also anchored within gunshot-range to windward. At about midnight on 7 August eight fireships were loosed on the Spanish fleet forcing them to cut their cables and escape to seaward.

It is difficult to understand what lay behind Parma's unreadiness. He had had plenty of warning of the Armada's approach; he had earlier told Philip that he was ready and waiting; and yet he had done nothing. Was it a fit of pique at the shared command when he had previously hoped for the glory of sole leadership? Was it concern at the selection by Philip of a man unversed in the arts of war to command the naval side of the invasion, a man moreover who was generally unpopular among the Spanish nobility? Had the months of waiting raised doubts in his mind over the feasibility of Philip's plan as a whole? There is no question that Parma was a man of great personal courage; he was the most brilliant and successful of all the Spanish generals, with the reputation of being able to solve all difficulties; and he could inspire his troops to follow him wherever he led them. It is difficult not to believe that by this time he had no intention of playing the part assigned to him in Philip's 'Enterprise of England' and that he had unilaterally withdrawn from the whole venture.

The dispiriting news from Dunkirk must have been almost the end of all Medina Sidonia's hopes. He knew that it was impossible for the Armada to remain in safety at Calais for a long time, and he had a very shrewd idea of the method that would be used by the English to drive it from its anchorage. Fire had been a naval weapon at sea since its introduction by the Byzantines in the seventh century, and the Spanish navy had used its modern equivalent of fireships only the previous year in an attempt to drive Drake out of Cadiz during the raid on that port. He ordered Captain Serrano to take a pinnace to windward of the fleet and be prepared to tow away any English fireships that might be launched against the Armada, and he warned every captain in the fleet to watch for such an attack and if need be to weigh their anchors or slip and buoy their cables so that they could return to the anchorage when the danger was past. Because of the strength of the tides, all the Spanish ships were lying to two anchors. Their spare anchors were stowed below decks, and this was to be a source of much trouble on the morrow.

Wynter claimed later that it was he who first suggested a fireship attack to Howard. This may be so, but the use of fireships to dislodge the Armada must have been in the forefront of the thoughts of every naval officer in the fleet. Howard called a council in the *Ark* and it was agreed to launch such an attack at about midnight, when the tide would be at mid-flood and running at its strongest. There was no lack of owners of the smaller merchantmen who wanted to volunteer their ships for the fire attack, knowing of course that the Queen would recompense them for their loss. Among the volunteer owners were Hawkins with the *Hope* of 180 tons and Drake with the *Thomas* of 200 tons. Six more were offered, the *Bark Talbot* (200 tons), *Bark Bond* (150 tons), *Bear Yonge* (140 tons), *Elizabeth* (90 tons), *Angel* (120 tons) and 'Cure's Ship' (150 tons). They were packed with faggots, pitch, gunpowder and other combustibles, and just after midnight were fired and sent off on their task, each towing a longboat astern for the escape of their crews at the last moment. They were commanded by Captain Yonge, owner of the *Bear*, and Captain Prowse, owner of the *Angel*. The cost to the Queen was agreed at £5,111 10s.

Medina Sidonia wrote in his *Relation*:

At midnight two fires were seen burning in the English fleet. These increased to eight, and suddenly eight ships with sails set, and wind and tide behind them, came direct towards our flagship and the rest of the fleet. All were burning

The night attack by fireships on the Spanish fleet at anchor in Calais roads. In the foreground a Spanish galleasse is being engaged, probably a loose interpretation of the events of the following morning when the galleass San Lorenzo was driven ashore.

fiercely. The duke, seeing that as they drew near our men did not arrest them, and fearing that they might be explosion vessels, weighed and ordered the rest of the Armada to do the same, designing when the fire should have passed by, to return and take up the same station . . . The current was so strong and drove our Armada in such a manner that although the flagship and several of the vessels near her anchored again and fired a gun, the rest did not see them and were carried as far as off Dunquerque.

Another Spanish officer wrote:

Every vessel was forced to shift itself thence as best it could, flying from so great a peril as that which stared us in the face . . . Fortune so favoured them [the English] that there grew from this piece of industry just what they counted on, for they dislodged us with eight vessels, an exploit which with one hundred and thirty they had not been able to do nor dared to attempt.

Most of the Spanish captains had lost their nerve at the sight of the advancing fireships. In their anxiety to get clear they had cut their cables instead of weighing or buoying them, and had lost their anchors as the result. When Medina Sidonia anchored and fired a gun as a signal for the rest of the Armada to follow suit, they had no anchors on deck with which to do so and they drifted away down to leeward ever nearer the coastal banks. During the confusion several ships fouled each other, with some damage to their yards and rigging. Only one of the ships was seriously damaged, but she was the *San Lorenzo,* the flagship of the galleasses, the largest and certainly one of the most important and powerful ships in the Armada. She drifted into the *San Juan de Sicilia,* one of the big Levanters, and lost her rudder. Unable to steer, her rowers beached her on one of the sandbanks in the harbour.

As dawn broke on the morning of 8 August the English could see, in the early morning light, the full result of the fireship attack. There was a small group of Spanish ships at anchor just out to sea from Calais, with more than half of the Armada streaming away down the Flanders coast and showing no signs of being able to rejoin. It was a situation tailor-made for an English victory. In his *Relation* Medina Sidonia reported that the wind had veered to the north-west, but this seems improbable, for with the wind from this direction the remainder of the Armada should have been able to tack and rejoin the flagship. English sources give the wind as south-south-west, which seems more likely as this would have put the Spanish flagship dead to windward of the rest of the Armada. It was at the same time a fair wind for the English fleet as it prepared to bring the whole weight of its attack on the isolated Spanish group. To windward of the group lay the *San Martin,* with, anchored a little way down to leeward, the *San Juan, San Marcos, San Mateo, San Felipe,* and about half a dozen other ships.

It was at this moment that Howard succumbed to the temptation that had assailed Drake during the night of 31 July when he left the fleet to capture a personal prize. As he was leaving Calais, Howard saw the *San Lorenzo* stranded in the harbour, and he led off in the *Ark* to capture her, most of the rest of his squadron following him. As the water was shallow he sent in his boats to attack and pillage her, obviously hoping that so important a ship would be carrying a good amount of gold and silver. There was little way he could have known that Parma's army was not already embarked and waiting for the Armada to arrive, and the evidence of his own eyes showed him the Spanish ships approaching Dunkirk, where he knew that Parma's army lay. At best his action was a foolish waste of time when so obvious a chance of victory offered; at worst it was a dereliction of his clear duty as Commander-in-Chief. Eventually the Governor of Calais took a part, claiming that the *San Lorenzo*, ashore in a French port, was under the jurisdiction of the King of France, and driving off the English boats with shot from the guns of the castle.

When Medina Sidonia saw the English ships leaving Calais he weighed anchor, with the intention of running downwind and forming a defensive concentration on the ships farthest to leeward so that he would have all the Armada around him. But his pilots warned him that such action would put the whole fleet in peril of running aground, and in the face of this advice he had no alternative but to stand and fight with his few ships, hoping to win enough time for the remainder to claw their way clear of the Dunkirk banks and make their way back to his assistance.

The English attack was led by Drake in the *Revenge*, his squadron following him in a formation resembling quarter-line. The *San Martin* was the nearest of the Spanish ships and she took the full brunt of the attack, the remaining ships of the group being still a little to leeward of her though beating up to come to her assistance. Normally with a ship separated from her fellows, the Engish tactic was to surround her and batter her into submission, but as Drake passed out of the smoke of battle he saw that about half of the Spanish ships that had been scattered to leeward along the coast had now won clear and were also working up towards their battered flagship. He led his squadron off to intercept them, leaving the *San Martin* and her small group to the attention of the other English squadrons following after him.

The *San Martin* had been considerably damaged and suffered heavy casualties in the attack by Drake's squadron, but by now the rest of her small group was approaching fast, as also were the English squadrons of Hawkins and Frobisher. Again it was the *San Martin* that received the first of the fire, both English squadrons trying to cripple her or force Medina Sidonia down towards the Zeeland banks. 'But', wrote one of his officers, 'he kept luffing up continually upon the enemy's fleet, transfigured and shrouded in the smoke of his guns, which he ordered to be fired with the greatest rapidity and diligence.' Some Spanish critics have blamed Medina Sidonia, holding that he should have run to leeward to re-form the Armada before risking an engagement, but in the face of his pilot's warning, it is difficult to see what other course was open to him. His actions did at least enable nearly half the Armada to make an offing from the coast and eventually to join him.

Drake had lost his race to intercept the approaching Spaniards, and by about ten o'clock in the morning there were some fifty or so ships in company with the *San Martin*. It was about now that Seymour's squadron reached the battle and Wynter reported the Armada, or such of it as had reached Medina Sidonia, as forming up 'into the proportion of a half-moon'. He continued:

> Their admiral and vice-admiral, they went in the midst and greatest number of them, and there went on each side on the wings their galleasses, Armada of Portugal [galleons] and other good ships; in the whole to the number of sixteen in a wing, which did seem to be their principal shipping.

The English tactic was to concentrate their squadrons on the windward wing of the Spanish formation, continually crowding it in on the centre and driving the Armada

The battle of Gravelines, off the Flanders coast, the decisive battle in which the Armada was finally defeated.
By this time the superiority of the English galleon design had been fully demonstrated, as it had enabled the fleet
to change its tactics from long-range gunnery to action at point-blank range.

down to leeward in an attempt to force it to the east of Dunkirk and make impossible its junction with Parma. The wind, increasing in strength and veering more westerly, was making it even more difficult for the Armada to win its way into the deeper water of the North Sea and safety from the shoals of the Dutch coast. In forcing the Armada to give way the English had forsaken their previous practice of long-range firing and now closed in to make every shot tell. As Wynter wrote to Walsingham on 11 August:

> I deliver it unto your honour upon the credit of a poor gentleman that out of my ship [*Vanguard*] there was shot 500 shot of demi-cannon, culverin, and demi-culverin; and when I was furthest off in discharging any of the pieces, I was not out of shot of their harquebus, and most times within speech one of another.

A Spanish officer confirmed Wynter's statement:

> The English ships, using their prerogative of nimble steerage, whereby they could turn and wield themselves with the wind as they listed, came oftentimes very near the Spaniards, and charged them so sore that now and then they were but a pike's-length asunder.

As the battle raged the Armada was about six miles to seaward of Gravelines and still being driven by the wind ever eastward. Time after time one or two of the Spanish ships were cut off from the main body and brought under devastating fire by as many as a dozen English galleons. They suffered fearful casualties and immense damage to their hulls, masts and rigging. The courage of the Spaniards was magnificent as they fought in their ships against such odds. The two ships most hotly engaged, apart from the *San Martin*, were the *San Mateo* and the *San Felipe*. Their captains were Don Diego Pimentel and Don Francisco de Toledo, and their valour was worthy of the flower of Spanish chivalry.

The battle lasted for eight hours throughout the day of 8 August. During the last few minutes the English managed to cut off from the rest of the Armada some fifteen ships, which included the *San Martin*, and it seemed impossible that they could escape. But as the English ships closed round for the kill a vicious squall swept down on the two fleets, accompanied by heavy rain which blotted out all visibility. The English ships rounded up into the wind to ride out the squall; the Spanish, too much damaged in masts and rigging to do the same, ran before the wind. When the squall had passed, it was seen that the Armada had managed to regain its close formation. Certainly the squall had robbed the English of a good handful of prizes, but at the same time it had cost the Armada one of its 'great Biscayans', the *Maria Juan*, which had sunk after being in collision with the *San Juan de Sicilia*. It had also driven the Armada to leeward of Dunkirk, and from the English viewpoint removed all danger of its making a rendezvous with Parma's invasion army.

During the night there were even more losses in the Armada. After the punishment they had received during the day's fighting the *San Mateo* and *San Felipe* were both too badly damaged to be made seaworthy. They were abandoned and drifted down to the Zeeland coast where they were taken by some of Justin of Nassau's ships and brought in to Flushing. Through some misunderstanding there were officers left on board both ships after their crews had been taken off, and among the prisoners taken from them by the Dutch were Don Diego Pimentel and Don Francisco de Toledo. One other ship went ashore and was lost but there is no record of her name. She was probably one of the smaller merchantmen.

Spanish seamen abandon ship during the battle of Gravelines on 8 August. The ship is either the San Mateo *or* San Felipe, *both of which were so badly damaged in the fighting that their crews abandoned them.*

Greveling Calis   Diever

The coming of the squall saw the end of the day's fighting; indeed, the end of all the fighting of the campaign. Although the English victory had not been crowned with the taking of several Spanish prizes, it was none the less a complete victory. All the objectives of the English fleet had been achieved. The Armada had been driven out of the English Channel, and its attempt to return had been frustrated in the morning's fighting. It had been unable to join forces with Parma, and in its final desperate attempt to seek safety in the deep water of the North Sea had been beaten back into the shoals of the Dutch coast. Many of the Armada's ships had been sorely damaged, some had expended all their shot in the fighting, and the casualties had been high. Captain Vañegas put the figures at 600 men killed and 800 men wounded; others had been picked up from the water and were now prisoners in English ships. No English ship had been lost and though several had been damaged they were still seaworthy and full of fight. In a letter to Walsingham, Thomas Fenner, captain of the *Nonpareil*, put the English losses, apart from losses by sickness, at not more than sixty in the whole campaign. Of other English estimates, the highest was less than one hundred men lost.

There was little change during the night except that the wind veered a little, coming fractionally from the north of west. Both wind and sea increased considerably, making the position of the Armada even more perilous in the shoaling water. 'Hardly a man slept that night,' wrote Padre Geronimo, one of the friars accompanying the Armada. 'We went along all wondering when we should strike one of those banks.' Only Medina Sidonia and a small group of two or three galleons, which included Miguel de Oquendo's *Santa Ana* and de Leyva's *Rata*, and one of the three remaining galleasses, shortened sail and luffed up as close to the wind as they could to try to stem the rush to destruction. The rest of the Armada captains were by now too demoralized to think of anything but to run from the English fleet no matter what other dangers lay ahead.

With daylight on the morning of 9 August it was seen that the *San Martin* and her small group were isolated, with the English fleet just about within gunshot. It was the classic situation so eagerly sought by the English ships during the campaign, to cut off a small group and surround it before the rest of the Spanish fleet could come to its assistance. Now the rest of the Armada was six miles away and still flying before the wind with all sails set. Medina Sidonia and his officers confessed themselves to their priests and prepared to sell their lives as dearly as they could. The English fleet approached, and then for some reason unknown to the Spaniards did not attack. The reason in fact was that many of the English ships were short of shot after the expenditure of the previous day and, in any case, if the wind held the entire Armada was certain to come to grief on the Zeeland banks.

When the English ships turned away, Oquendo and de Leyva brought their ships close to the *San Martin* to implore Medina Sidonia to attack. To do so might have been a fine despairing gesture but it made no sense when the rest of the Armada was so far out of reach. Oquendo and de Leyva accused Medina Sidonia of cowardice and worse, but he stood firm, unwilling to shed more Spanish blood through useless defiance. His pilots sounded the depths and found they had six fathoms; where the *Patrona*, one of the galleasses, did the same she had but five. And still the same wind blew, strong and relentless, towards the banks. Don Luis de Miranda, one of the military officers on board, wrote: 'It was the most fearful day in the world, for all the people

A view of the fortifications at Great Yarmouth. From about 1586 most of the south and east coast ports of England had fortifications erected to meet the threat of invasion by a Spanish army from the Netherlands. Great Yarmouth contributed the Grace, *a merchant ship of 150 tons, to the English fleet for the Armada battles.*

The Spanish galleon San Mateo, *commanded in the Spanish Armada by Don Diego Pimentel, one of Spain's most notable sea captains. He remained on board after the crew abandoned the ship, and he was captured by the Dutch when the* San Mateo *drifted ashore.*

were now in utter despair of a happy issue and stood waiting for death.'

Surprisingly, a 'happy issue' came at the very last moment. The wind began to back, first a point or two to west-south-west and then swung, according to some of the English accounts, right through to the south-east. This may well be so, as the squally weather of the previous day points to a drop in barometric pressure and, as most seamen know, a wind in the south-east accompanied by low pressure indicates stormy conditions for a period of several days. Certainly, as the Armada was to find to its cost, the following days were beset with storms. But wherever the wind, it freed the Armada from the Zeeland banks, blowing it into the deeper water of the North Sea.

The Spaniards attributed the change of wind direction to the direct intervention of God, but it still raised some awkward questions for the Spanish leaders. A wind from the south-east was a fair wind for a return to Dunkirk and Parma's army, or to the English Channel where the ships might find shelter and replenishment. Medina Sidonia summoned a council of his leading officers on board the *San Martin* and put his problems before them. The most serious was the present condition of the ships. There was also concern that provisions and fresh water were not only perilously short but going putrid; and in addition to the wounded there were some 3,000 sick among the crews. The council, after considering and rejecting a proposal to make for Hamburg

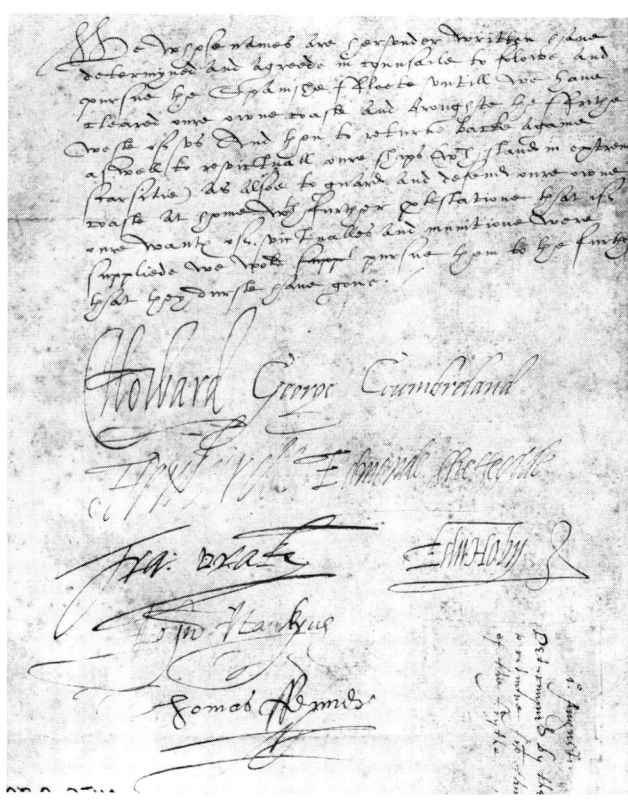

to refit and continue the campaign, recommended a return to the English Channel. No one spoke up for Dunkirk, having lost faith in Parma's ability to get his army ready for the invasion. But against this decision lay the English fleet, still undefeated and still able to fight, and an attempt to re-enter the Channel would certainly be bitterly contested. It was not a prospect of much promise after the experience of the previous day. Again the wind took a hand, hauling round to the south and increasing, kicking up a vicious sea. A return to the Channel was still possible, but only just. The council changed its mind and recommended that the ships should head for Spain round the north of Scotland. There was now no stomach for yet another fight with the English and the duke, accepting final defeat, led the Armada seaward on a northerly course.

Howard also called a council on board the *Ark*. Obviously he had not appreciated the magnitude of the English victory off Gravelines, nor did he realize the extent of the damage to the Spanish ships or their lack of ammunition. 'Sir,' he wrote to Walsingham, 'I will not write unto her Majesty before more be done. Their force is wonderful great and strong; and yet we pluck their feathers by little and little.' It was of course much more than that and, had he but known it, the Armada was in fact no longer a fighting fleet but a defeated and demoralized rabble. The council, fearing that Medina

The resolution signed by the principal officers of the fleet after the battle of Gravelines, committing themselves to pursue the Armada as far north as the Firth of Forth and then return to defend the English coasts. It is signed by Lord Howard of Effingham, Lord Thomas Howard, Sir Francis Drake, Sir John Hawkins, Thomas Fenner, the Earl of Cumberland, Lord Sheffield, and Sir Edward Hoby, Howard of Effingham's secretary.

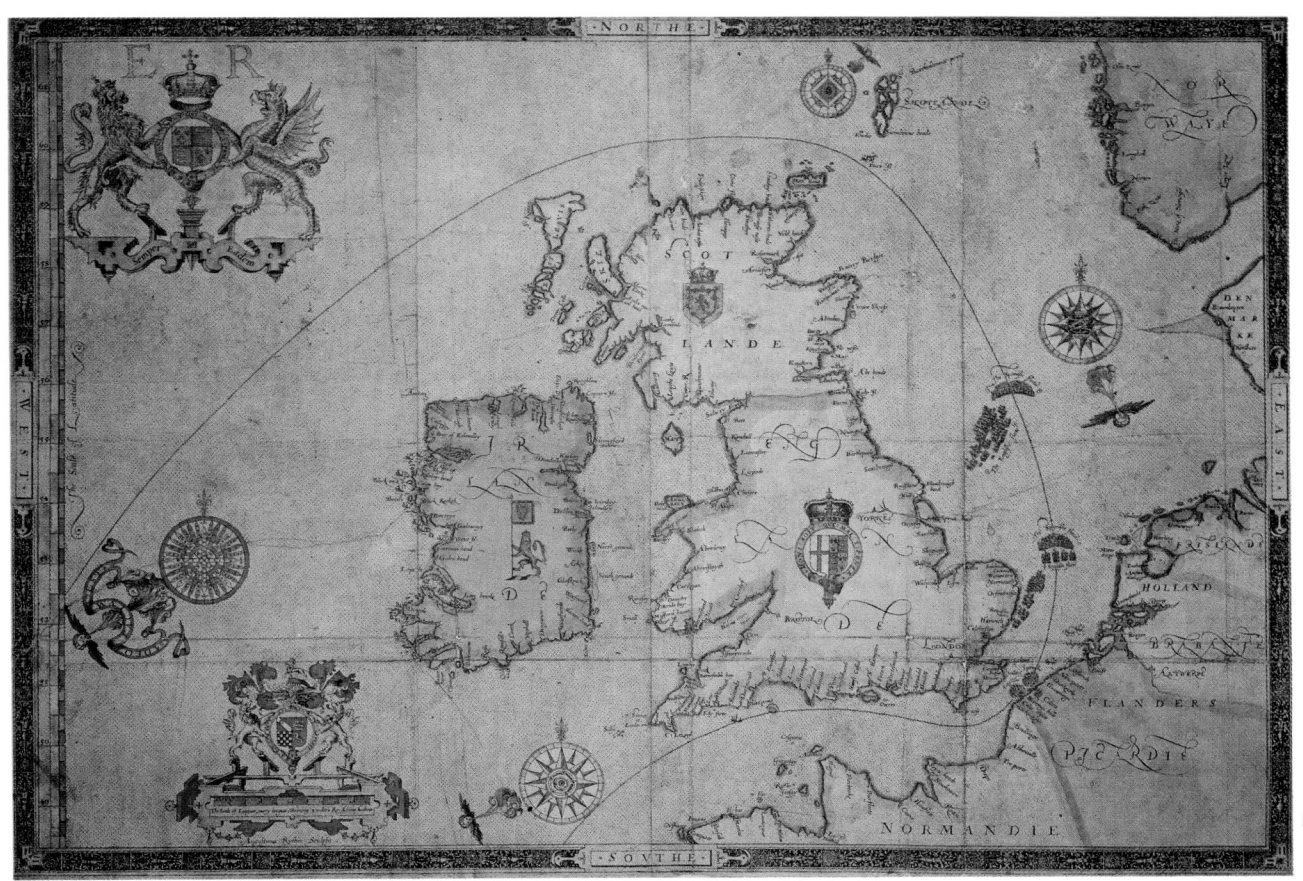

The track of the Spanish Armada. Some of the Spanish ships may have sailed as far west as shown on this chart, but most of them sailed through the Minches between the Hebrides and the mainland.

Opposite: Queen Elizabeth inspecting her army at Tilbury. Although the Armada had by this time been driven north to Scotland, the English troops remained encamped to oppose a possible invasion by the Duke of Parma's army.

Sidonia might be planning an attack on Scotland, decided to follow the Armada up the North Sea as far as the Firth of Forth. It also decided to detach Seymour and his squadron, much to that nobleman's disgust, to the Downs to continue his watch on Dunkirk and Parma's invasion army. As Seymour wrote to Walsingham:

> I pray God, my Lord Admiral did not find the lack of the *Rainbow* [Seymour's flagship] and that company; for I protest before God, and have witness for the same, I vowed I would be as near or nearer with my little ship to encounter our enemies, as any of the greatest ships in both armies; which I have performed to the distress of one of their greatest ships sunk [possibly the *Gran Grin*] if I have my due.

Medina Sidonia had by now officially abandoned the whole campaign. On 11 August he sent off a despatch to Philip setting out his reasons for giving up. His Invincible Armada was almost destroyed by the better gunnery and seamanship of the English fleet; his best ships had no more shot for their guns; he was of the opinion that he would best serve his King by trying to save the fleet by taking the northerly course home, although his pilots had no knowledge of the perilous waters. 'God', he wrote, 'has seen good to direct matters otherwise than we expected.' As the Armada sailed north Medina Sidonia ordered that all the horses and mules embarked in the ships be hoisted up on deck and driven overboard in order to preserve the dwindling supply of drinking water. It made very little difference, for even before the ships passed between the Orkney and Shetland Islands, many men were dying of thirst.

When the English fleet reached the latitude of the Firth of Forth, it turned back and left the Armada to its fate. Both Howard and Drake detached a pinnace from their squadrons to keep in touch in case the Armada should return to try to make contact with Parma, though neither believed it possible or likely. By then the Armada no longer existed. It had lost its formation, with individual ships attempting to make their own way home to Spain through the stormy waters of the north. Many of the English ships were also by now in poor shape from lack of provisions. Victuallers sent out from east coast ports to replenish the fleet had been unable to find it, having had no more direction on where to look than to search towards the north-east. It was high time the English ships looked to themselves, for sickness among the crews was growing.

As the ships returned they put into various ports along the coast from Harwich to the Downs. Drake anchored in Harwich, Howard in Margate. There he found a letter from Calais awaiting him, telling him that all Europe was ringing with the story spread by Don Bernardino de Mendoza of a great and disastrous defeat of the English fleet. Howard wrote to Walsingham:

> Sir, in your next letters to my brother Stafford [Sir Edward Stafford, English ambassador in Paris] I pray write to him that he will let Mendoza know that her Majesty's rotten ships dare meet with his master's sound ships; and in buffetting with them, though they were three great ships to one of us, yet we have shortened them 16 or 17; whereof there is three of them a-fishing in the bottom of the seas.

As he laid his pen down his attempt to put the record straight must have given him considerable satisfaction.

10 The Sorrowful Return

As the two fleets disappeared from the North Sea, the English into their ports on the east coast, the Spanish into the wild waters of the North Atlantic, the people of Europe waited for news. The future lay in the balance. A Spanish victory would mean a Europe mainly under Spanish dominion, half a continent held in thrall to the inquisitorial doctrine of Roman Catholicism and the torture and burnings of heretics. Even more important, the prizes of America and of India and beyond would be grasped firmly in the hands of Spain.

The last view of the Armada had seen it still on course for the north of Scotland, but one day later a westerly gale would have made it possible for it to seek a Danish or Norwegian port where it might refit and return to the Channel and Parma. On 20 August Drake wrote to Walsingham that he considered this to be Medina Sidonia's most likely course of action, as he could not think that the Duke would be so mad as to attempt a return to Spain northabout with so many crippled ships in his fleet. He also warned Walsingham not to forget Parma. 'I take him', he wrote, 'to be as a bear robbed of his whelps', and thought him likely to take any desperate course to retrieve his shattered reputation.

England and Spain were almost as much in the dark as the rest of Europe, for until the position of the Armada was rediscovered, anything might happen. So, in the void of any reliable information, rumours sprang up and spread, and there was no more avid spreader of rumour than Don Bernardino de Mendoza. Throughout the years of preparation for Philip's 'Enterprise of England' he had been Spain's political spider sitting in the middle of the web, serving his master by arranging the checks and balances necessary to achieve Philip's dreams of empire. Like Burghley in England he had built up a wide network of spies and informers, and he was at the centre of a highly organized messenger service to spread the Spanish story to all the European capitals. It is not known where the first story originated of the English defeat in the Channel, which had so upset Howard as he was approaching Calais, but it was certainly Mendoza who spread it throughout Europe.

Some confirmation of this original story reached Mendoza by way of a group of Breton fishing vessels, returning from the Newfoundland cod fishery. On reaching Le Havre they reported that they had passed through a great naval battle in the Channel. That simple piece of information grew in the telling, and Mendoza's agent in Rouen reported that one of the skippers had seen fifteen English galleons sunk during the battle and others captured. From Dieppe came another report that one of the other skippers had seen the *Revenge* attacked by a Spanish galleasse, which brought down

Don Bernardino de Mendoza, the Spanish ambassador in Paris during the planning and execution of the 'Enterprise of England'. Philip II made him privy to all his plans and relied on him to generate support for Spain throughout Europe.

A procession of the Holy League in Paris in 1590. The League, a Roman Catholic association, was heavily financed and armed by Philip of Spain as a means of obtaining Spanish control of France.

her masts with the first broadside and sank her with the second. He had also seen Drake escaping from the wreck of his flagship in a small boat.

Without pausing to wonder how a group of small fishing vessels could remain so long in the midst of a naval battle or how they could have observed so much detail through the gunsmoke which surrounded the fighting ships, Mendoza sent this new version around Europe as confirmation of the previous story. At the same time he ordered a huge bonfire to be built in the front courtyard of his embassy, to be lit in celebration of the victory of the Spanish Armada as soon as he had a further report from his agent in Rouen.

But there was a much bigger fish to fry first. The future of France as an independent nation depended on an English victory, for without it the Holy League under its Guise leaders would become the dominant power in France and Henry of Guise was already in Philip's pay and pocket. The report of a Spanish victory in the Channel, if true, gave Mendoza the lever he needed to force the Valois King to embrace the Holy League and thus acknowledge the claim of Henry of Guise to succeed him as the next King of France, binding the nation firmly to the policies and ambitions of Spain. He requested an audience at the palace at Chartres, to which the King had been forced to retreat after Guise had outfaced him in Paris.

Mendoza's meeting with the King did not go as well as he had hoped. On the strength of his victory report he suggested that it would be in order for the King to call for a celebratory *Te Deum* to be sung in all French cathedrals and churches and that it would be well for him to demonstrate his approval of this Catholic crusade for the restoration of the true faith by returning to Paris, his capital city. This would deliver him into the hands of the Guise faction and achieve Mendoza's main objective. The King, however, had other sources of information. He handed Mendoza a letter he had received from M. de Gourdan, the Governor of Calais, telling how the Armada had arrived there with the English fleet in hot pursuit, how it had been dislodged by the attack of the fireships, and how, the following morning, the English fleet had been seen chasing it into the North Sea. Mendoza returned unhappily to Paris, deciding that he must wait a little longer before igniting his bonfire.

The next item of information to reach Mendoza was more worrying. The captain of a Danish merchant ship reported that he had sailed through a mass of swimming horses and mules in the North Sea, with no ships in sight to explain the phenomenon. They were of course those which Medina Sidonia had jettisoned to save the consumption of drinking water. Even Mendoza realized that they could only have come from the Armada. The position given by the Danish skipper showed that the Armada must have been some hundreds of miles north of its rendezvous with Parma and apparently on its way to Scotland. It was all very puzzling because Mendoza, who was privy to the planning of the whole operation, knew well that Scotland did not figure in Philip's plans for the Armada.

A week later an even more extraordinary rumour made its way around Europe. It may have owed its origin to the return of some twenty-five ships of the English fleet to the mouth of the Thames after chasing the Armada to the north. Other groups of ships had put in to other east coast ports from Harwich southward. Some observers may have assumed that the twenty-five were all that remained of the fleet, which indicated that a battle must have been fought somewhere in the North Sea in which the English fleet had been heavily defeated. Mendoza seized on this notion, announced the date of the battle as 13 August, and claimed the loss of some twenty English galleons sunk or captured, with others so damaged by Spanish guns that they had perished in a storm that had followed the action. Indeed, had it not been for the storm, Spanish ships would have chased and accounted for the twenty-five which had succeeded in reaching the Thames. The Armada was now, he suggested, refitting in a Scottish port and would soon be on its way back to Flanders and the rendezvous with Parma's army.

Mendoza's messengers spread this story throughout Europe. It reached Count Olivarez, the Spanish ambassador in Rome, a few days later and he lost no time in relaying it to the Pope, reckoning that enough time had elapsed since the date of the battle for the Armada to have returned and landed Parma's army in England. As well as demanding that a victory *Te Deum* be sung in St. Peter's, he reminded Sixtus V of his promise of a million gold ducats when the first Spanish soldiers set foot in England and suggested that a substantial first instalment was due. The Pope agreed, if it were all true, but it would be advisable to wait for confirmation of this report.

Over the next week or so the story was much embroidered. Presumably because among the twenty-five English ships in the Thames was neither Howard's *Ark* nor Drake's *Revenge*, then both must have been lost in the battle. So rumour had it that the *Ark* had been captured and the *Revenge* sunk after attempting to carry the *San Martin* by boarding. Drake's reputation in Spain as the most fearsome of all the English seamen obviously required a really dramatic conclusion and this new story now had him as Medina Sidonia's prisoner on board the Spanish flagship.

It was all too good to miss. Mendoza lit his victory bonfire in front of the Paris embassy and his messengers once more took to Europe's roads. Again Count Olivarez visited the Vatican, but after the dusty answer he had received on his previous visit he was now more circumspect. No one could have hoped more for Spanish success than the Pope, but, as he told Olivarez, he had different information. He had had a report from Flanders, probably based on the interrogation of Don Diego Pimentel, that the English had won a great victory, and another report from Venice where it was said that the Duke of Parma had broken up the camp at Dunkirk and withdrawn his army. It was better to await the full truth before accepting any of the stories.

In Spain Mendoza's report was received with rapture, particularly the news that Drake was now Medina Sidonia's prisoner. Juan de Idiáquez, the King's principal secretary, had it printed as a broadsheet, translated into various European languages, and circulated throughout Europe. Inevitably some copies found their way into England where they caused much official indignation. The Privy Council had by now received official reports of the fighting from Howard, Drake, Seymour and others, and it knew, too, that no English ships had been lost. The Spanish report was translated into English and, with the English version of the fighting opposite it paragraph by paragraph, was published as a pamphlet with the title *A Pack of Spanish Lies*. Even as it reached the streets of London it had been overtaken by the truth in Paris. Burghley had circulated a shortened version of Howard's official report, *Abstract of Accidents between the Two Fleets*, and Stafford had had it translated into French and printed in Paris as *Discours Véritable*, to become one of the first authentic accounts of the campaign. As the first copies were being circulated, terrible news was arriving out of Ireland, a fearsome story of Spanish shipwreck, of starving crews, of men dying of thirst, of the wholesale massacre of survivors. There could be no mistaking its truth, and Europe at last knew of the completeness of the English victory.

The title page of A True Discourse, *an account of the Armada battles based on Howard of Effingham's report and first published in Paris by the English ambassador to counter rumours of a Spanish victory.*

An aerial view of Dunluce Castle on the northern coast of Ireland. It was owned at the time by Sorley Boy McDonnell, who ruled over north-east Ulster. Five survivors from the shipwrecked Girona were captured and taken to Dunluce Castle.

As the English fleet turned south and left the Armada on 13 August, Medina Sidonia took stock of his situation. He knew he had passed the point of no return so far as the Channel and Parma were concerned, and the English fleet was still somewhere in the North Sea. He had lost seven good ships and a merchantman or two, and the rest of his best fighting ships had been so torn by the English broadsides that it was as much as they could do to keep afloat. Losses in killed and wounded had been so severe that most of the Armada ships were now under-manned. He knew that the morale of the fleet was dismally low, and he could do little to restore it. He had already punished the disobedience of his orders to stand and fight at Gravelines by hanging one of the delinquent captains and committing another nineteen to the custody of Don Martin de Aranda, the Judge Advocate General. Worst of all, in the light of the long voyage home, was the shortage of provisions and fresh water. All the fresh food secured at Calais had been consumed, most of the salt meat and fish had gone putrid, and much of the water was slimy and undrinkable. He ordered a daily ration throughout the Armada of half a pound of biscuit, one pint of water, and half a pint of wine. That was all, and even on that meagre allowance the Armada would need fair winds for Spain and a quick passage if the ships were to reach home without the crews dying from starvation and thirst.

On 17 August Medina Sidonia's pilots reckoned that they had reached the latitude of 61° 30′ North and that a south-westerly course would take the Armada safely through the waters separating the Orkney and Shetland Islands. Already some of the

Opposite: The Giant's Causeway, Co. Antrim, Ulster, where the Spanish galleasse Girona was wrecked when she was driven ashore and struck Spaniard's Rock.

ships had given up. Three of the big Levanters, very low in the water, had been seen breaking away to the east as though in search of a sheltering port in Denmark or Norway. They were never seen again. A sudden squall on the 17th scattered the squadron of hulks, notoriously bad sailers, and one of them, the *Gran Grifon*, went ashore on Fair Isle, between the Orkneys and Shetland. Juan Gomes de Medina, admiral of the squadron, and his crew remained there throughout the following winter. After the squall passed it was followed by rain and a drop in temperature, and cold became another enemy to be endured for there was no spare clothing for the crews.

The Armada still had the worst of the voyage before it and none of the pilots had sailed the waters before. There was almost continuous bad weather, and two heavy storms took a sad toll of the struggling ships. We can get some picture of the hardships endured from the interrogation of prisoners taken from the subsequent wrecks on the Irish coast. Even in the best provisioned ships three or four men died from hunger or thirst every day, and many more from sickness. A prisoner from the *San Juan*, one of the galleons of Castile which left her bones on the Irish coast, told that more than 200 men on board had died before she was wrecked.

It is difficult to identify the individual disasters which struck the Armada during its voyage down the coasts of Scotland and Ireland. It was no longer proceeding as a fleet, having been split up into small groups and even ships on their own. The stormy weather and battle damage both affected the speed and sailing performance of individual ships. It is known that at least nineteen were lost by shipwreck or sank within sight of shore, but another thirty-five failed to return to Spain and their fate is unknown. Alonso de Leyva, the King's favourite, who had been appointed to command the Armada if Medina Sidonia were killed or otherwise incapacitated, was on board the *Rata Coronada* when she was wrecked on the coast of Erris. He was saved and taken on board the *Duquesa Santa Ana*, only to be wrecked again in Glennagiveny Bay, near Inishowen Head. Once again he was saved and transferred to the galleasse *Girona*. She was lost when she struck a rock near the Giant's Causeway, still known as Spaniard's Rock, and de Leyva went down with the ship. Five men struggled ashore and were taken to Dunluce Castle. The *Nuestra Señora de la Rosa* was wrecked among the Blaskets. The *San Marcos*, *San Juan*, *Trinidad Valencera* and *Falcon Blanco Mediano* are among those known to have ended their lives on the Irish coast. There were many others. Perhaps the most unfortunate ship of all was the *San Pedro Mayor*. She escaped the dangers of the Scottish and Irish coasts and reached the mouth of the English Channel. There she lost her way and was wrecked in Bigbury Bay on the coast of Devonshire.

The treatment of survivors from the wrecks in Ireland was nothing less than barbarous. Those who managed to get ashore with money or valuables of any sort were robbed by the local Irish (in the interrogation of prisoners the robbers were described as 'savages') and even their clothes were stripped from them if they were wearing embroidered coats, satin or velvet breeches, or leather boots or shoes. They were then picked up by soldiers and put to the sword by command of the English provincial governors. If any appeared to be men of some consequence they were kept in prison in case they might prove worthy of a ransom. Typical of the reports from Ireland was that of Sir Richard Bingham, the Governor of Connaught. In a letter to Walsingham he records that twelve ships came ashore on the coast of his province: 'And so I can say, by good estimation, that 6 or 7,000 men have been cast away on these coasts, save some 1,000 of them which escaped to land in several places where their ships

DRAVN AFTER THE QVICKE

A contemporary drawing showing the reception of shipwrecked Spanish seamen by Irish peasants. Although a few of the Spaniards who struggled ashore were killed by the peasants, the vast majority were rounded up and put to the sword by the English garrisons of the Irish provinces.

fell, which sithence, were all put to the sword.' There was no mercy shown even in their great extremity.

On 22 September, the *San Martin* staggered into Santander, with 200 dead on board and the remainder starving and sick. Over the next two weeks another sixty or so ships made their way home to Spanish ports, some in a worse condition even than the *San Martin*. There was no money to pay off the crews, no food or clothing or medical supplies to relieve their needs, and scurvy and typhus flourished in the ships to add to the grisly death toll. Of the 130 or so ships that had set sail from Corunna in July, sixty-three had failed to return, and of those which did, more than a dozen had to be broken up as beyond repair. One of the ships which reached port was wrecked at the very end of her perilous voyage as she had no anchor left on board to bring herself to a stop. Estimates of the exact number of ships lost vary considerably, ranging from forty-one in one account to sixty-five in another. The figure of sixty-three is that arrived at by Captain Fernandez Duro, whose work on the Armada published in Madrid in 1885 was based entirely on the Spanish State Papers.

If, as Drake had suggested to Walsingham, Parma might embark on a desperate venture on his own to restore his reputation, the danger periods would come with the spring tides of the September equinox. Without them there was insufficient depth of water for his transport barges to get out to sea. When it was known in London that the English fleet had returned, the Queen was anxious to pay off the ships to save the continuing drain on the Treasury of keeping them in full commission. She was dissuaded by the uncertainty over Parma's actions. Even when the spring tides had passed, the uncertainty remained and the ships were kept in commission for another four weeks until the end of October.

But the English fleet, scattered in its various ports down the east coast, was in trouble. The men were kept on board in increasingly insanitary conditions, short of food and prey to diseases. An epidemic of typhus was raging through the ships and men were dying in alarming numbers. And because the ships were lying in different harbours and not together as a fleet in a naval port, the administrative system broke down. We get a picture of their desperate plight in a letter from Howard to Walsingham, written from Dover on 29 August:

> It were too pitiful to have men starve after such a service. I know her Majesty would not, for any good. Therefore I had rather open the Queen Majesty's purse something to relieve them than they should be in that extremity; for we are to look to have more of their service; and if men should not be cared for better than to let them starve and die miserably, we should very hardly get men to serve. Sir, I desire but that there may be double allowance of but as much as I give out of my own purse, and yet I am not the ablest [wealthiest] man in the realm; but before God I had rather have never penny in the world than they should lack.

It was all sorted out in the end and all the bills were paid, but it took a long time, and the seamen who had made the victory possible were a long way back in the queue for payment. It is sad to have to record that there were a great many who died of disease and starvation before they could receive their due reward.

When the King of Spain finally learned the full extent of the Spanish disaster he called the European ambassadors to the Escurial to assure them that he would build a new and yet stronger fleet to renew the 'Enterprise of England' the following year. There may have been some people in Spain who believed it possible, but in the rest of Europe there were few, if any, who did. For most people the defeat of the Armada had been something of a miracle, and had broken for good the back of Spanish sea power.

A gold salamander set with jewels, found in the wreck of the galleasse Girona.

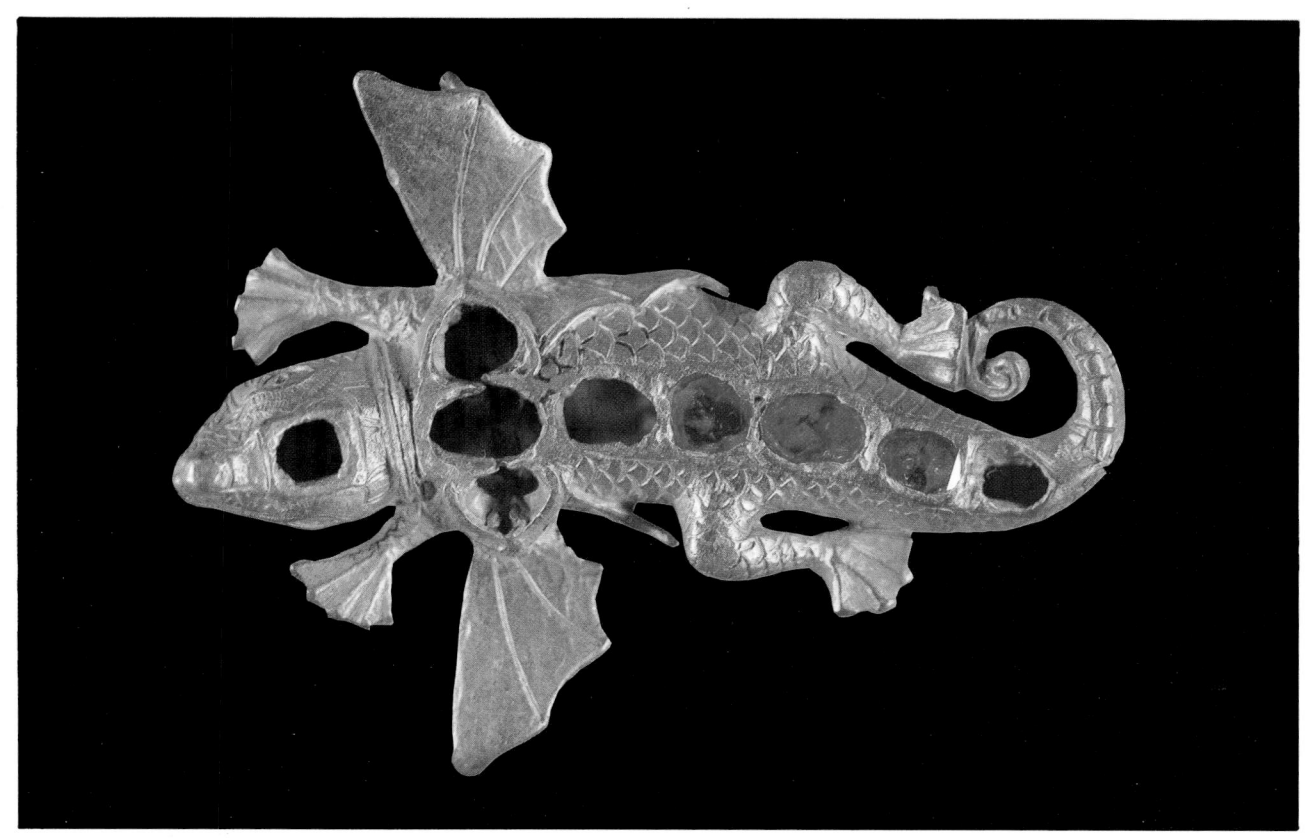

LISBONA.

OLISIPO, SIVE VT PERVE-
TVSTÆ LAPIDVM INSCRIP-
TIONES HABENT, VLYSIPPO,
VVLGO LISBONA FLORENTIS-
SIMVM PORTVGALLIÆ EMPORIV.

Cum Privilegio.

CASCALE Lusitaniæ est.

Berbelerm

11 Lisbon 1589

Although England rejoiced in the victory over the Armada, although there was a feeling of national pride in the way the admirals, captains, officers and men had fought and triumphed, there was also a feeling of disappointment. True, it was accepted as a great victory, but apart from a few captured Spanish banners hanging in St. Paul's Cathedral in London, there was little to show for it. Beyond the *Rosario* and the *San Salvador*, there were no ships captured and brought in as prizes, no worthwhile plunder of treasure and plate to set against the huge cost of the campaign.

For Drake, the events of the Armada formed an unfinished story. It was an article of his fighting faith to do battle in the enemy's waters rather than in one's own, and it made strategic sense to him to try to capitalize on the success of 1588 with an expedition to complete the destruction of the maritime power of Spain in its own sur-rounding seas in 1589. It was already too late to think it possible in the remaining months of the present year.

Drake planned his expedition around the person of Don Antonio, still Pretender to the kingdom of Portugal and now a refugee in England. The years had not dulled his ambitions to wear a crown and he insisted that his presence in Portugal would rally at least 3,000 fighting men to his cause and that with English naval support Lisbon could be captured in his name.

The most distinguished soldier in England at that time was Sir John Norreys, whose experience had been gained in France in the Huguenot wars, in the Irish wars, and in the Netherlands under the flag of the Prince of Orange. Drake found him eager to join as commander of a military force if a new expedition against Spain were organized. Together they went to the Queen with their plan. Drake knew that if the Queen accepted it as a national venture the command must by right go to the Lord High Admiral, Howard of Effingham. But Drake had had a disagreement with Howard, for he believed that the report on the Armada that Howard had given to the Privy Council had not made enough mention of Drake and his deeds. So, to keep the overall command in his own hands, Drake proposed that the expedition should be undertaken on the old pattern of a joint stock company with the Queen as a principal shareholder. Her contribution to the company was to be six ships and two pinnaces, arms and armour for the troops, a siege train, four months' provisions, and £20,000 in cash. Drake and Norreys each agreed to contribute £20,000 and the balance would come from the city of London and various merchant adventurers. The Queen accepted the proposition on 29 October, the Privy Council empowered Norreys to visit the Netherlands to recruit additional support in ships and men, and Drake threw himself into the task

Opposite: A view of Lisbon in the sixteenth century. It was from Lisbon that the Spanish Armada had sailed in 1588 and it was to Lisbon that Drake hoped to sail in 1589 to complete the destruction of Spanish sea power. Because of a disagreement between Drake and Sir John Norreys, his military commander, the venture was a fiasco.

Overleaf: The Armada Jewel, a locket of gold, enamel, diamonds and rubies presented to Sir Thomas Heneage, Vice-Chamberlain of the royal household, on the defeat of the Spanish Armada. The profile bust of Queen Elizabeth on the outside of the locket and the miniature of her inside it (actual size 3·9 cm. high) are by Nicholas Hilliard.

A Spanish sea astrolabe found on the shore at Valencia Island, Eire, in 1845. Since astrolabes, instruments for measuring the altitude of the sun, were replaced by the more efficient cross-staff during the sixteenth century, it seems fairly certain that this must have come from one of the Armada ships.

of arousing London's financial enthusiasm with all his usual energy.

It grew quickly into a major expedition, larger in fact than the Queen had envisaged when she gave her original consent. Some gentlemen of her Court, possibly by her persuasion, withdrew their original support, but the magic of Drake's name and reputation more than made good their desertion. Within a fortnight of his arrival at Plymouth from Dover, where his ships had assembled, the nominal list numbered over 23,000 men, English and Dutch, of whom 17,000 were soldiers, 4,100 were seamen, and 1,500 were gentlemen adventurers. In addition to the Queen's ships were some sixty English armed merchant ships and sixty Dutch flyboats which Drake had rounded up off Dover. As they were sailing with Spanish passes it seemed probable that they had been tempted by promises of financial rewards to join forces with Spain and that they were destined for the new Armada which Philip had already announced. Drake looked upon them as legitimate prizes. With a little persuasion on his part their captains agreed to join his fleet.

Drake's intention was to sail directly to the estuary of the River Tagus, land the troops at Cascais, and use them to attack the three fortresses which commanded the seaway to Lisbon while he took his ships up to the city. But the Queen had other plans. The ships of the Armada which had reached home were still in Santander and other ports along the Biscay coast, and she wanted them destroyed before Lisbon was assaulted. Her instructions reached Drake well before he was ready to sail, and if he protested there is no existing record of his doing so. But the change of plan proved to be a mistake.

The expedition, delayed for three or four weeks by contrary winds and the perennial difficulties of collecting and embarking stores for so large a force, sailed from Plymouth on 28 April with Don Antonio and his suite embarked. Although it did not reach the nominal figures of its first muster, it was still a very large force of between 140 and 150 ships and some 16,000 men. There is no doubt that from the start Drake had been hoping and expecting to command a combined force that would compare well with the Spanish Armada of the previous year, and as the expedition put to sea it was only in the number of soldiers embarked that he was short of the Armada total.

Off the Biscay coast of Spain the wind was found to be unfavourable for Santander and the expedition assaulted Corunna instead. After some brisk fighting the town was subdued, the shipping in the port destroyed or taken in prize, the local cattle rounded up and slaughtered as additional victuals, and the surrounding countryside laid bare. Unfortunately one of the warehouses in the captured lower town contained many casks of wine collected for the new Armada and resulted in widespread drunkenness among the soldiers and sailors, and indeed many of the officers. This wine, still probably in a raw state, was later blamed for the subsequent disastrous losses from sickness.

The English assault on Corunna alerted the Spanish authorities, and in particular Philip's viceroy in Lisbon, to the danger of an English raid led by the still formidable Drake. In Lisbon the viceroy rounded up the known supporters of Don Antonio and hanged them, and marshalled the citizens into defensive militias. The element of surprise, on which Drake had relied for success, was destroyed. 'If we had not been commanded to the contrary,' he later wrote to Walsingham, 'but had first landed at Lisbon, all would have been as we could have desired it.'

Leaving Corunna, the expedition sailed down the Atlantic coast of Spain towards the River Tagus and Lisbon. Once again the flaw which had plagued so many Elizabethan naval ventures showed itself. Learning from a passing merchant ship that a large Spanish Indiaman had put into Peniche, some fifty miles by road from Lisbon, Drake could not resist the temptation of a rich prize. The little port was found to be in a state of defence, the soldiers were landed, and after three or four hours of fighting the town capitulated. But the Indiaman was gone; she had sailed three days earlier.

This episode led to a disagreement between the naval and military commanders. Drake wanted to re-embark the soldiers and follow his original plan of landing the troops at Cascais. But with his troops now ashore, Norreys wanted them to march the fifty miles to Lisbon where, with the 3,000 armed supporters promised by Don Antonio, he was confident of taking the city. Each failed to convince the other. Drake sailed with his ships to the Tagus and captured Cascais; Norreys set off on the march to Lisbon, finally reaching the suburbs of the city though with the loss of about a thousand of his men from exhaustion and sickness. It was not the first time, nor was it the last, when the naval and military commanders in a combined operation were unable to agree on the correct strategy and thereby turned possible success into utter failure. Norreys was held in the suburbs of Lisbon by the determined resistance of Philip's viceroy; Don Antonio's promised 3,000 fighting men failed to materialize; and sickness was decimating Norreys's forces. After a few days of stalemate he was forced to retire to Cascais.

Drake lay at Cascais, awaiting word from Norreys that he had captured Lisbon. As no word came, he decided to try to force the passage up river with fifty of his best ships, leaving the remaining hundred at Cascais. It meant running the gauntlet

of the fortresses that commanded the river, but without soldiers to attack them from the land it was a risk he felt he had to take. As he was about to sail, a messenger arrived from Norreys with the news that the army was in retreat. There was now nothing left for Drake but to await the arrival of Norreys and embark him and his men.

A decision to attack the Azores was aborted because of unfavourable winds, and eventually the fleet straggled home, much scattered by storms. One bonus was the capture of some sixty Hanseatic ships laden with corn and contraband of war destined for the new Armada, and when they were brought home they were sold for £30,000. Although the expedition had failed in its major tasks, it had still cost Spain dear in destroyed and captured ships and in the loss of a great many new guns captured at Corunna. It had also cost England a prodigious number of lives lost from sickness in the fleet and the army. Of the 16,000 men who sailed from Plymouth, no more than about 6,000 were brought home.

William Camden, the great contemporary historian, summarized the expedition. 'Most certain it is', he wrote, 'that England was so far a gainer by this expedition, as from that time to apprehend no incursions from Spain, but rather to grow more warm and animated against that country.' Perhaps so, but the object of the expedition had been to deal a final death blow to the maritime power of Spain and in that it had failed utterly. And because of that failure the naval war with Spain was to drag on for many more years.

Queen Elizabeth I, the 'Armada Portrait', by George Gower. She is shown resting her hand on a globe, representing English mastery of the seas after the defeat of the Spanish Armada. The two panels show (left) the English fleet in chase of the Armada, and (right) a Spanish ship wrecked on the coast.

Sir Francis Drake

Reuiued :

Calling vpon this Dull or Effeminate Age,

to folowe his Noble Steps for Golde & Siluer,

By this Memorable Relation, of the Rare Occurrances
(neuer yet declared to the World) in a Third Voyage,
made by him into the West-Indies, in the Yeares 72. & 73.
when *Nombre de Dios* was by him and 52. others
only in his Company, surprised.

Faithfully taken out of the Reporte of Mr. *Christofer Ceely*, *Ellis
Hixon*, and others, who were in the same Voyage with him.
By *Philip Nichols*, Preacher.

Reviewed also by Sr. *Francis Drake* himselfe before his Death,
& Much holpen and enlarged, by diuers Notes, with his owne
hand here and there Inserted.

Set forth by Sr. *Francis Drake* Baronet
(his Nephew) now liuing.

AVXILIO · DIVINO

SIC PARVIS MAGNA

LONDON
Printed by *E. A.* for *Nicholas Bourne* dwelling at the
South Entrance of the *Royall Exchange.* 1626.

12 Balance Sheet

Flavit Deus et dissipati sunt, 'God blew with his winds and they were scattered', has been accepted for too long as a reasonably accurate description of the events of the voyage of the Spanish Armada. The Latin tag is found on statues of some of the principal English naval leaders and as an inscription around many of the medals struck to commemorate the event. Sometimes the words vary though they all mean the same thing.

This description arose from a desire on each side to show that the Almighty favoured its particular cause. When the wind changed at the end of the battle of Gravelines and saved the entire Armada from complete disaster on the Zeeland banks, it was held by the Spaniards as a direct intervention by God and thus proof that their cause was also the cause of God. When the storms broke off the coast of Ireland and drove so many Spanish ships to their destruction, those who supported the Reformation saw it as proof that God was a Protestant. It was a convenient philosophy under which all could shelter, one to excuse any shortcomings or failures of the administrations ashore or of the admirals and captains afloat.

Nothing of all this, of course, can be further from the truth. When the wind changed at Gravelines the Armada was already a defeated fleet that had lost its cohesion, its morale, and its discipline. Nearly half its ships were too heavily damaged to fight again, the captains of the remainder were no longer prepared to obey the orders of their Commander-in-Chief. When the stormy winds off Ireland drove so many Spanish ships ashore, the majority of them had been in the thick of battle and were too much damaged to hold their way against the westerly storms.

The campaign at sea had, in a way, been a struggle between the mediaeval and the modern world. The outdated galley mentality of the Spanish fleet, the military rather than the naval command of ships and squadrons, the cumbersome design of their ships, were all powerful factors in the Spanish defeat. For the first time the Spanish fleet was up against a professional navy, whose ships had the priceless advantage of a technical break-through in hull design. The advantages were apparent in each of the three actions fought in the Channel, when the English were able to gain the advantage of the weather gauge and always managed to win their way clear of danger.

The English tactic of avoiding close action during the Channel battles and relying on their longer range culverins to harass the Spanish ships was a measure of caution against the largely unknown fighting qualities of a considerable enemy fleet. It was also a realization that, during these battles, the Armada enjoyed a considerable numerical advantage in ships; it was not until Seymour's squadron joined the fleet at Calais that the numbers were approximately equal. There was another consideration. All the

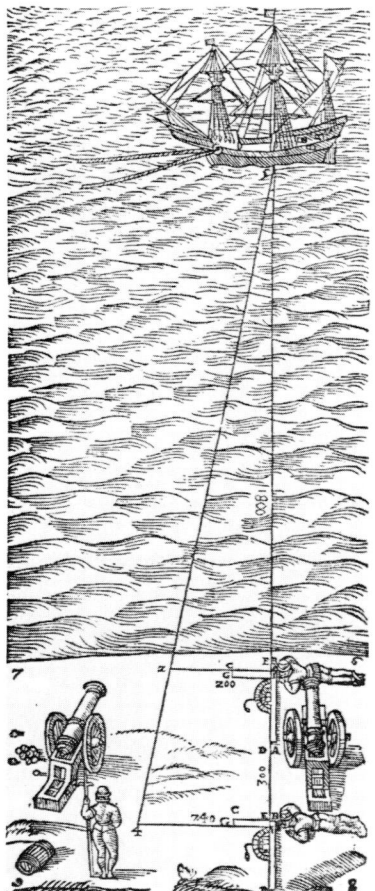

A page from Tartaglia's
Colloquies on Artillery,
*illustrating the method of finding
the range of a ship at sea.
Disappointed by the lack of
decisive results achieved by
English gunnery during the
Armada battles, naval leaders
decided to concentrate on the
training of ships' gunners, based
on Tartaglia's principles.*

English commanders in the Channel, Howard, Drake, Hawkins, Frobisher, commented on the immense size of many of the Armada ships, particularly the galleasses. In a letter to Walsingham, Howard wrote: 'Some made little account of the Spanish force by sea; but I do warrant you, all the world never saw such a force as there was.' We know that the disparity in size was nowhere near as great as the English thought; the Spanish ships merely looked great and powerful because of their extensive cage-works, the high-charged fore and aft castles. By the time of Gravelines, when the English leaders had the measure of the quality of the Spanish ships, they closed the fighting range to less than a hundred paces, about eighty yards, in order to do the maximum damage with their guns. They no longer feared the danger of the Spanish ships coming alongside and the crews attempting to board, as they knew from experience that their own ships had the speed and the agility to keep clear of such close encounters.

After the fighting the main talking point of those who had taken part in the Armada battles was the small amount of damage done to the enemy ships by the English gunfire. Only at Gravelines, and in one or two episodes in the Channel when a Spanish ship had been cut off and surrounded, had damage been significant. The reason was attributed to two main causes, a shortage of trained gunners and the fact that at long range the shot lost too much of its initial velocity to penetrate when it hit. Some held that it was lack of powder which explained the failure to destroy the Armada during the chase up the North Sea after Gravelines; others, more percipient, that the shortage of powder was caused by the gunners wasting so much in indiscriminate firing before making sure that their guns were properly directed at the target.

The results of these deliberations were twofold. The first was a proposal to revive Henry VIII's Fraternity of Artillery, responsible for manning and training. 'If it had pleased God', ran the opening paragraph of the proposal, 'that Her Majesty's ships had been manned with a full supply of good gunners . . . it would have been the woeful-lest time or enterprise that even the Spaniard took in hand.' It was recommended that the complement of gunners in each type of warship be increased by one-third; Cyprian Lucar's translation and editing of Tartaglia's *Colloquies on Artillery* was endorsed as a training manual; and it was further proposed that an allowance of powder be made available from the Government's stores for exercise in gunnery.

Although no mention was made in this proposal of an ideal range for battle, the admirals and captains made their own decision. A Tudor ship's gun consisted of a loose-fitting ball in a brass cylinder with black powder as the only propellant, and naval leaders had come to realize that long-range firing was an inevitable waste of powder and shot. From the Armada experience stemmed the adoption of short-range battle, so beloved by British admirals of the future. It is an oddity of naval history that, after the Armada, Spanish and, later, French admirals and captains always opened their actions at long range, hoping to bring down masts and yards to cripple their enemy before he could get within 'half pistol shot', at which every shot could be made to count.

One other legacy of the Armada was the question of the value of armed merchant ships as additions to the fleet. Almost to a man the English naval leaders considered them to be of little use. Wynter, in a letter to Walsingham written after the battle of Gravelines, echoed the general opinion. 'I dare assure your honour', he wrote, 'if you had seen that which I have seen of the simple service that hath been done by the merchant and coast ships, you would have said we had been little holpen by them

A Dutch print of 1598 of Queen Elizabeth as Europa. Her right arm is made up of Italy, her left of England and Scotland, and her feet rest on Poland. Above her head is the defeated Spanish Armada, on the right a triple-headed Pope is rowed away by clergy escorted by ships representing the papal allies.

otherwise than they did make a show.' It was not that merchant ships were any less armed or any less willing than the Queen's ships, it was purely because the navy had become more professional and had developed a pattern of tactics into which the untrained merchant ship no longer fitted.

From that realization followed the inevitable conclusion that maritime power in the future must rest on the maintenance of a regular navy of sufficient size to maintain the command of the Narrow Seas and to foster the national ambitions of expansion of trade and wealth in distant waters. It was no longer realistic to rely on a nucleus of royal ships bolstered up by merchantmen to carry the burden. It was decided to increase the size of the Navy from the approximately thirty existing ships to fifty, most of the new ones to be built to a tonnage of over 700. We can perhaps see the hand of Drake in the decision to build the new ships on the lines of the *Revenge*, his flagship in the Armada battles and always his favourite ship.

The reaction in Spain to the disaster of 1588 was to build a new fleet, partly to replace the Armada losses but also to provide a better protection for the treasure *flotas* from America and the East. The result of the Armada itself had been to let loose a flood of English privateers in American waters, which so overwhelmed the Spanish defence that on many occasions the sailing of the *flotas* were postponed for as much as a year or more for fear of falling into English hands. Spain also built a squadron of galleons based on the new English design, for operations in the Narrow Seas of the Channel and the Bay of Biscay. Certainly Spanish sea power was revived considerably over the next fifty years or so with all the new construction, but it was always over-extended by Spain's continuing ambitions to widen her control over Europe.

The succession of the Huguenot Henry of Navarre to the throne of France after the assassination of Henry of Valois, suggested to Philip the opportunity of adding France, and with it the chance of controlling the English Channel, to the Spanish power in Europe. With the design of defeating Henry and replacing him with the Guise faction, he used his new fleet to occupy parts of Brittany as a base for further operations against the Navarre king and, later, against England. But the plan miscarried. English ships and English forces which Elizabeth despatched to the aid of the French king drove the Spanish forces out of Brittany, and Henry of Navarre adopted the Catholic faith on condition that he was crowned in Paris. And so the stalemate continued.

The long grumbling war between England and Spain rumbled on for all the years that remained to Elizabeth. It had its ups and downs on both sides, and if Spain never regained the dominance at sea which she had once enjoyed, neither did England establish the mastery which the Armada victory should have made possible. Perhaps it needed a new and younger naval leader of the calibre of Francis Drake to replace the ageing English admirals, a man with Drake's vision of strategy and mastery of tactics, but no such man came forward during these years. Drake himself, held responsible for the failure at Lisbon, was in disgrace, and even Elizabeth, once his great admirer and protagonist, could not shrug off the failure and promote him over such old faithfuls as Howard, Hawkins, and Frobisher. The torch of English sea power had to await the coming of a new generation of English seamen before it could flame into its full brilliance.

A Note on Sources

The State Papers of all the countries concerned are the main and essential sources of contemporary information on the Armada campaign. The English State Papers are in the Public Record Office, London, those of other countries in similar central collections of national archives. The English naval documents for Drake's Indies voyage of 1585–6 and his raid on Cadiz in 1587 have been collected and edited by Sir Julian Corbett in *The Spanish War* (Navy Records Society, 1898); and for the events of 1588 by Sir John Laughton in *State Papers Relating to the Defeat of the Spanish Armada* (Navy Records Society, 2 vols., 1894–5). The Spanish State Papers covering the same period have been similarly collected and edited by Captain C. Fernandez Duro in *La Armada Invencible* (Madrid, 1885). The English State Papers dealing with aspects of the campaign as seen and reported from foreign countries, and those similarly concerned with domestic aspects, are all in the P.R.O. and have been skilfully calendared. The Calendar of State Papers, Foreign, XXI and XXII, and the Calendar of State Papers, Domestic, II, 1581–90, are those which include the reports on the campaign in their particular fields. There is a small collection of Spanish documents, including some letters from Philip II, in the National Maritime Museum, London. They have been translated and included, together with Petruccio Ubaldino's second and longer account of the campaign of 1588 (see below), in George Naish's *The Naval Miscellany*, Vol. IV (Navy Records Society, 1952). The French Archives Nationales contain copies of Mendoza's correspondence.

The earliest English account of the campaign of 1588, apart from interim letters or 'despatches' from individual commanders at sea, is an unsigned and undated manuscript in the Cottonian Collection in the British Museum. It is a narrative written by Howard when the fleet returned after chasing the Armada up the North Sea. It is included in Vol. I of Laughton's Navy Records Society publication. Also in the British Museum is an Italian translation of it, dated 15 April 1589, by Petruccio Ubaldino, a Florentine historian who came to England as a young man and was employed by various noblemen. It is dedicated to Howard, and that dedication makes clear that Howard asked Ubaldino to translate it into Italian, though for what purpose is not apparent. Bound up with it, but virtually unnoticed until recently, is a longer narrative in the same handwriting. Howard's narrative makes very little mention of Drake's part in the fighting, probably stemming from his displeasure at Drake's abandoning the fleet during the night after the first action off Plymouth in order to take the *Rosario* as a prize. After Ubaldino had translated Howard's narrative, either he must have approached Drake or Drake approached him for a fuller version to be written to include

Drake's part in the battles. This was completed on 12 August 1589 and Ubaldino sent a copy of it to the Grand Duke Ferdinand de Medici at Florence, the original being presented by Ubaldino to Sir Christopher Hatton, the Lord Chancellor, who was one of Drake's principal backers in his earlier voyages. Ubaldino's translation of Howard's narration was re-translated into English and published for Augustine Ryther, a notable engraver of charts, in 1590 under the title *A Discourse concerninge the Spanish Fleete invadinge Englande in the Yeare 1588 and overthrowne by Her Majesty's Navy under the Conduction of the Lord Charles Howarde, High Admirall of Englande*. It contained the eleven charts of the movements of the two fleets drawn by Robert Adams which became the basis of a series of tapestries designed by Cornelisz Vroom and commissioned by Howard to hang in the House of Lords. They were destroyed in the fire of 1834. In 1919 the Roxburghe Club published *Lord Howard of Effingham and the Spanish Armada*, a handsome volume of John Pine's engravings of the Armada tapestries, with an introduction by Henry Yates Thompson.

A large number of contemporary broadsheets, newsletters and pamphlets circulated in various European countries. They add little to our knowledge of the events of 1588 and all that can really be said about them is that they reflect, to some extent, the national hopes and anxieties throughout Europe concerning the outcome of this titanic struggle.

Of modern accounts, the outstanding analysis of the Armada campaign remains Sir Julian Corbett's *Drake and the Tudor Navy*, 2 vols. (1898). It needs to be read with a degree of caution as Drake was Corbett's great hero, above all other admirals, and this shows. Nevertheless, in its description and analysis of the Armada battles, it remains the classic account. The Tudor background to the naval development of the period is admirably brought out in A. L. Rowse, *The Expansion of Elizabethan England* (1956) and J. A. Williamson, *The Age of Drake* (1938) and *Hawkins of Plymouth* (1949). In the historiography of Elizabethan England the student ignores at his peril the work of Sir John Neale, not only for his biography of the great Queen but also for his studies of her Parliaments, diplomacy, and finances. His work throws a bright and penetrating light into the sometimes obscure darkness of the Tudor policies during Elizabeth's years. Other publications of much value in the political and diplomatic sphere are L. Cabrera de Cordoba, *Felipe II, Rey de España* (1877), R. B. Merriman, *Philip the Prudent* (1934), Conyers Read, *Mr Secretary Walsingham*, 3 vols. (1925) and Leon van de Essen, *Alexandre Farnese* [Duke of Parma], 5 vols. (1937).

The most recent work on the Armada is Dr Garrett Mattingley's *The Defeat of the Spanish Armada* (1959), a monument of infinite research and fluent interpretation. If to some readers it appears to spend more time in exploring the European byways rather than the mainstream of the Armada epic, it is none the worse for that.

There are several contemporary lists of the ships involved in both fleets among the national archives of both nations. There are small variations between most of them but it is possible to reach reasonably verifiable totals. It can be said with some confidence that the total number of ships engaged on the English side was 197, of which fifty-eight were small unarmed coasters used only to carry replenishments of victuals and ammunition to the fleet as it made its way up Channel. It can be said with equal confidence that the strength of the Spanish fleet when it left Corunna was 130 ships, of which the four galleys which accompanied the Armada never reached the English Channel.

It is also possible to be reasonable sure of the number of men embarked, as both the English and the Spanish Admiralties kept records of Victualling and Pay lists. There were 15,925 men embarked in the English ships, including the replenishment coasters, and 29,453 in the Armada, including 1,250 men in the four galleys which were forced to seek shelter in the Bay of Biscay.

Figures of the tonnages of the ships in both fleets are far more suspect and can only be taken as very approximate. England and Spain used different formulae in calculating tonnage, the Spanish formula enhancing the tonnage in some cases by as much as 25 per cent. On an average of the individual ship tonnages from all contemporary sources, the figure for the English fleet comes out at 28,906 tons and that for the Spanish fleet at 57,868 tons. Allowing for the enhanced figure produced by the Spanish measurement formula, a more realistic figure of 43,401 tons is reached. But to this must be added a tonnage for the four galleasses. Because their hull form was based on the galley design there was no measurement formula on which their tonnage could be estimated, but they were certainly the largest and most heavily armed ships in either fleet. These aggregate figures do not necessarily mean that the Spanish ships were larger than the English ships, an opinion which has been widely held over the years. The English *Triumph*, Frobisher's flagship, was certainly as big as the largest Spanish ship apart from the galleasses. But the figures do indicate that in ships of the middle range, from about 400 to 700 tons, the Armada outnumbered the English fleet in a ratio of about eight to one.

It is impossible to do more than speculate on the number of guns mounted in each fleet. Spanish figures in the contemporary lists show a total of 2,431 guns in the Armada ships. In the English lists only the guns mounted in the Queen's ships are given; the number mounted in the merchant ships can only be estimated as a guess based on the tonnages of the ships. Such a guess gives an approximate total English figure of about half the Spanish. But even if roughly correct, the figures still have little meaning as the proportions of large guns to small is indicated nowhere in the records. The best modern work on this tangled subject is Professor Michael Lewis's 'Armada Guns' in *The Mariner's Mirror*, Vols. XXVIII and XXIX (1942–3).

Index

Acknowledgements

The publishers wish to thank the owners, museums, galleries, libraries, photographers and others who have contributed towards the reproductions in this book.

Aerofilms Ltd: 133; Archivo General de Indias, Seville: 28; Archivo Iconografico, SA, Barcelona: 55, 103, 115; Ashmolean Museum, Oxford: 135, 149; Bodleian Library, Oxford: 109 (photo: Bridgeman Art Library); Bridgeman Art Library: 34, 43, 124; The British Library: 8, 17, 49, 82, 102, 110, 121, 123, 148; Courtesy of the Trustees of the British Museum: 147; John Carter Brown Library, Brown University, Rhode Island: 66–7; Folger Shakespeare Library, Washington: 88–9, 131; Giraudon: 14, 22; Courtesy of the Hispanic Society of America, New York: 20, 24; The Louvre, Paris: 44, 51, 68 (all photos: Lauros-Giraudon); By permission of the Master and Fellows, Magdalene College, Cambridge: 31, 34 (photo: Bridgeman Art Library), 35, 36 left, 71, 104; The Mansell Collection, London: 16, 85, 93; Mas, Barcelona: 6, 9, 10; Musée Carnavalet, Paris: 50, 128–9 (photos: Giraudon); Museu de Marinha, Lisbon: 122, 138; Museo Maritimo, Barcelona: 2–3 (photo: Archivo Iconografico); Museo Naval, Madrid: 72, 73; National Galleries of Scotland, Edinburgh: 47; National Maritime Museum, London: 36 right (photo: Bridgeman Art Library), 40, 42, 100, 105 (photo: Bridgeman Art Library), 107, 113 (photo: Bridgeman Art Library), 125 (E-T Archive), 142; National Portrait Gallery, London: 63; Picturepoint Ltd: 132; City of Plymouth Museums & Art Gallery: 27, 56, 62, 86, 146; The Prado, Madrid: 59 (photo: Archivo Iconografico), 77 (photo: Scala); Public Record Office, London: 61; Rijksmuseum, Amsterdam: 23, 80; Royal Armouries, HM The Tower of London: 87; By kind permission of the Marquess of Salisbury, Hatfield House, Herts: 39, 65; Society of Apothecaries, London: front cover, 116–17; By kind permission of the Marquess of Tavistock, and the Trustees of the Bedford Estates: back cover, 19, 144; Tiroler Landesmuseum, Innsbruck: 97 (photo: Archivo Iconografico); Ulster Museum, Belfast: 137; Universitätsbibliothek, Cologne: 53; Victoria & Albert Museum, London: 140–1 (photo: E-T Archive)